LIFE AND TRAVEL IN

TARTARY, THIBET, AND CHINA:

BEING A NARRATIVE OF

The Abbe Huc's Travels in the Far East.

BY

M. JONES,

AUTHOR OF "THE BLACK PRINCE, A BOOK FOR BOYS,"
"KANE, THE ARCTIC HERO," ETC.

WITH THIRTY-THREE ILLUSTRATIONS.

London:
T. NELSON AND SONS, PATERNOSTER ROW.
EDINBURGH; AND NEW YORK.

1885.

Preface.

GREAT book is said to be a great evil. The Abbé Huc's account of his travels in Tartary, Thibet, and China, is certainly not a very large book; and yet, for young readers, it may with advantage be made less. So, by choosing here and there, and compressing the portions that I select, I have brought some interesting details of life in those little known regions into small compass. This mode of proceeding has, of course, compelled me to trust to my own vocabulary, to the exclusion of his admirable one, in relating the experience of himself and his colleague. It is right to mention this, that the Abbé may not be held responsible for my manner of narrating his facts.

The missionaries were of course Roman Catholics. But it is only right to say that they evidenced a true Christian spirit throughout the whole of their difficult, toilsome, and hazardous enterprise.

M. J.

LONDON, 1867.

Contents.

LIFE AND TRAVEL

IN

TARTARY, THIBET, AND CHINA.

CHAPTER I.

SETTING OUT.

CHINA, Tartary, and Thibet, are countries still so little known, that any fresh information about them from those who have travelled there in earnest is always acceptable. The Abbé Huc's account of his journeyings in some of the most inaccessible and out-of-the-way portions of these out-of-the-way places, furnishes details so novel and full of life, that we have selected it to assist us in giving our young readers some slight idea both of the people and the lands which he visited.

The circumstances of his going thither were these: At an early period Christianity had been introduced into China by French missionaries,—members, of course, of the Roman Catholic Church. Their efforts were, for a time, attended by great success; but at

length persecution arose of so severe a character as
almost to extinguish the light that had shone amid
the thick darkness around. Numbers of the converts
fled for their lives into the wilds of Tartary, where,
gradually, some order and union among them were
effected; and the few Christians who dared to remain
in Pekin, the capital, were thence directed and

PEKIN.

governed by the missionaries, who still clung to their
charge. Brighter times succeeded; and in 1844 the
Abbé and his companion, the Abbé Gabet—who had
taken up their dwelling in the Valley of Black Waters,
situated in that part of China called Mongolia—determined on undertaking a mission that should pene-
trate still further into the heathenism by which they
were surrounded.

It was on an autumn morning in that year that the small cavalcade which composed the expedition was in marching order at the door of the missionaries' dwelling. It consisted of the Abbé Huc on horseback, Gabet perched on a tall camel, their sole attendant, or servant of all work—a native Christian, who, oddity as he was, was much attached to his masters—and two camels laden with the scanty stores for their journey, among which a tent and copper cooking-pot were included. Prayers were first offered, and then they took their departure, the Chinese Christians accompanying their pastors for a mile or two, and then leaving them to pursue their rugged path across a high mountain, to the inn where they were to rest the first night. The landlord of this inn, who, in the high-sounding phraseology of the Chinese, was called Comptroller of the Chest, was one of their own converts, so they were sure of a kindly reception on that occasion.

Inns similar to this one are found dotted here and there in the Tartar wilds bordering upon China. A high wattled enclosure surrounds a mud building ten feet high, and chiefly consisting of one large, dirty, smoky, ill-smelling room, that serves for all purposes —cooking, eating, and sleeping also; that is, for those who are not too fastidious to sleep in Tartar bed-rooms. In the centre of this room, and nearly filling up the entire space, is the travellers' portion of the accommodation, called the *kang*—that is, a kind of stove raised about four feet from the rest of the floor, the surface of which, covered with a mat, affords a warm seat for the guests, who squat upon it cross-legged, drinking everlasting- tea, smoking, gambling, quarrelling, fighting, according to their various tastes. Three great coppers set in this stove do the cooking for the establishment, the viands being prepared and

KANG OF A TARTAR-CHINESE INN.

handed about by the people of the house, to whose sole use that portion of the floor not occupied by the *kang* is dedicated. So goes on the business of the day : at nightfall all is changed. Such of the sojourners as have bedding with them, spread it on the still warm *kang*, and take their luxurious repose in that fashion ; those who are less fortunate, lie down

on it "all standing," as the sailors say, sometimes
packing themselves in two circles, feet to feet, to
economize space. And thus, amid the feeble glimmer
of an evil-odoured lamp in a broken tea-cup, they
resign themselves to sleep.

The missionaries declined availing themselves of
this snug accommodation. They had made up their
minds to travel as Tartars, and so were for roughing
it at once, under their own tent. This was accordingly
set up, their goat-skins unrolled beneath it for beds,
a good fire of brushwood lighted (for the nights were
cold), and, just as the night-drum was being beaten,
causing the valleys to resound with its brazen clang,
and frightening the tigers and wolves around out of
their senses, they dropped happily asleep, for they had
to be up and off betimes. Previous to their departure,
however, some important work had to be done—no
less than that of turning themselves from what appeared to be Chinese merchants, into travelling Tartar
Lamas. It seems that during the times of persecution
in China, the missionaries had felt themselves compelled, for safety, to adopt the ordinary dress of
Chinese laymen. As they were now, for a religious
purpose, going among the Tartars, whose decided
opinion it was that none but priests had any business
to talk about religion, Huc and his friend had determined on assuming the every-day dress of the
Lamas—that is, the Buddhist priests of the country
—such as they wore when not engaged in special
priestly functions. This dress also was the one worn
by their servant; who in his early youth had been
bred up for a priest, though, the college discipline of

the Lamas not being to his taste, he had, at the age
of eleven, taken French leave of his masters, and
vagabondized his way about the world until his con-
nection with the missionaries. Samdadchiemba—
such was his long and rather unpronounceable name,
which we hope was contracted to *Sam* for travelling
purposes—was short in stature, ugly, and very con-
ceited ; but, on the other hand, he was prodigiously
strong, and, as has been said, devotedly attached to
his masters; further, the poor lad, when it came to
the pinch, was a good Christian, in his way.

The first act in the metamorphosis of Chinese
merchants into Tartar Lamas, was, by one fell
stroke, to cut off the long pig-tails which had for
years adorned the backs of their heads—a proceeding which drew tears from some of their converts of
the inn. Nothing daunted, the change went on.
A long, wide-sleeved, yellow garment, buttoned at one
side with five gilt buttons and girded by a red sash,
was assumed ; over it came a red jacket with a purple
velvet collar ; a yellow skull-cap, with a red tuft at
top, surmounted the whole—which was a costume far
from unbecoming. Tartars in dress, they must also
be Tartars in all their habits. " Take away the wine
and the chafing-dish ! " was their exclamation when,
according to Chinese custom, the hot rice-wine (for
there wine is drunk hot instead of cold) and materials
for smoking were offered them : both tobacco and
wine being prohibited to good Lamas. The two
Abbés laughed at the complete transformation they
had undergone ; but their compassionate Chinese
disciples looked at them in silent dismay, doubting

not that their kind instructors were going to certain
destruction in the wilds of Tartary. Some bread
and wild fruit, plucked as they walked, made the
slight breakfast of the two; after which, with their

THE MISSIONARIES IN THEIR LAMANESQUE COSTUMES.

servant and camels, they fairly set forth on their
travels into wild and hostile lands, sustained and
comforted by the thought of their errand into those
dreary regions, which was to make known the name
of God where as yet it had never been heard. Their
only guides were a compass and a French map of

the Chinese Empire, of which Tartary and Thibet are
tributaries.

A rough rocky path up a mountain—famous for
the severity of its frosts, the wild beasts that haunt
it, and the bands of robbers who lurk in its defiles—
brought them to their next night's resting-place, a
grassy, tree-encircled spot, where, finding fuel and
water were to be had, they unloaded the camels and
pitched their tent, at whose door a great dog in their
company, named Arsalan, stood guard.   Fuel being
collected, consisting of dry branches of trees and
other waifs and strays, the kettle was soon set
a-boiling, and an attempt followed to manufacture a
species of soup of flour paste, like macaroni, and
some scraps of bacon. But, alas! this was one of
their failures: filling, each man, the little wooden
cup that forms an invariable part of a Tartar's equip-
ment, the mess was found absolutely uneatable, even
by hungry men in a Tartar desert; the very dog turned
up his nose at it!   Salt, salt, salt—fiery salt—was
the one predominant flavour of the nauseous com-
pound; salt not to be mitigated down to the eating
point—at least for the two Frenchmen—even by
soaking the acrid stuff in cold water and then boiling
it up again. Two small loaves and a walk in the
surrounding forest, which fortunately yielded a little
wild fruit to flavour the bread, formed their supper,
and they retired to rest well satisfied in one respect—that they had escaped the robbers of the Good
Mountain; for such is its rather inappropriate name.

These highwaymen of the Good Mountain have a
happy way of carrying on business.   In more

civilized countries, "gentlemen of the road" resort to
the coarseness of "Your money or your life!" or
something else equally explicit and compulsory.
Here, the victim is addressed with blandest courtesy:
"Venerable elder brother, I am on foot, pray lend
me your horse;"—"It is cold, oblige me with the loan
of your coat." And it is only when politeness of
this extreme kind fails of its intent, that the more
stringent persuasives of beating or sabring the
recusant into compliance with the request, is re-
sorted to.

The poverty and wretchedness of the country
through which the travellers wended their weary way
was striking; the more so that it had been brought
about to some extent by the gold and silver mines
in which it abounds, these having, as usual, drawn to
them all the floating vagabondage of the country,
whose only care was to ransack its treasures, leaving
the tillage of the ground to any who might choose
to undertake the thankless toil. In another district
of this miserable country, the contest waged between
the authorities and the twelve thousand rogues and
vagabonds who had betaken themselves to mining,
ended in a pitched battle between the two. The
miners, being defeated, fled for refuge to their mine,
the recesses of which proved no safety to them, as
the entrance to it was instantly blocked up with great
stones by the conquerors, who left their victims to
perish thus fearfully. Chinese cruelty was surely
satisfied for once.

In this evil district the fears of the travellers were
by no means allayed by their stumbling upon a party

of Chinese soldiers, encamped there for the preserva-
tion of the public peace, of which they themselves
were the greatest disturbers.   A quiet nook, however, apart from them, was fortunately found for the
night-halt; Gabet's horse and the servant's mule
were tethered at the tent door, the camels kneeling by
them so as to form a sort of barricade; and, after
the inevitable tea, for which Samdadchiemba had a
perfect enthusiasm, the party lay down to rest, and,
though sleepless, were undisturbed by thieves and
vagabonds either in or out of uniform.

The tea to which the Tartars are so passionately
attached, is not much like either what we in Europe
get or the Chinese themselves use.   For home con-
sumption and European export the small tender leaves
of the plant are carefully selected and dried.   The
coarse leaves and tendrils pressed into a mould till
the mass looks like a brick for building purposes, are
quite good enough for the Tartars and less civilized
Russians.   Their mode of making tea also differs from
ours :—A piece of the brick is knocked off, beaten into
powder, and boiled in a kettle until the liquid looks
red; salt is then added, and after the effervescence
which it causes has subsided, and the fluid is nearly
black, milk is poured in.   On high days and holidays
a quantity of butter is mixed with it, and it then
becomes a dish fit for a king !

CHAPTER II.

THEIR next day's ride brought the travellers to *Tolon-Noor*, a large, irregular, exquisitely dirty city, of most depressingly dreary environs, but of much importance both from the number of its population and the large amount of commercial business transacted in it. Russian commodities are brought here by way of Kiatka, a town on the northern frontiers of China, and which is the great point of communication between the two countries. Here the Russians and Chinese meet to exchange their goods; and through this town also passes the ten-yearly caravan of students going and returning between St. Petersburgh and the Russian convent at Pekin, maintained by the two governments for the education of Russian subjects as Chinese and Tartar interpreters. To Tolon-Noor from Russia and China come linen, tobacco, and tea: the Tartar brings his camels, oxen, and horses in exchange. The Chinese, in whose hands is the chief trade of the place, rapidly make fortunes here, and then return to their own "Celestial Empire" to spend them. The poor Tartars are as inevitably ruined. It is the old game of "head, I win; tail, you

(347)   2

lose," carried on on a large scale. The name of the city, not to be found on the map, signifies "Seven Lakes."

RUSSIAN CONVENT AT PEKIN.

The people of this town are celebrated for their foundries of brass and bronze. Statues, bells, and vases, used in the worship of Buddha are here manufactured, of excellent workmanship, for all the countries where that particular species of idolatry is practised. The worshippers of this false god are supposed to number four hundred millions. One statue of Buddha, a present to the Grand Lama himself—he is the high-priest of Buddha and supreme ruler of Thibet—was constructed of so great a size that its various parts, cast separately to be afterwards soldered together, formed a load for six camels! A small

bronze figure of our Lord, which the missionaries gave
them to copy, was reproduced with all the exact fidelity of the original, from which it was scarcely to be
distinguished.   It was done quickly and cheaply too.
Lamas abounded in this head-quarters for the manufacture of their "implements of devotion," and the
travellers held frequent conversations with them on
religious subjects, endeavouring to give them some
notion of Christian truth.   The priests took all that
was said very quietly, winding up with the exceedingly tolerant remark, "Well, we don't suppose ours
are the only prayers in the world."

Hotel life at Tolon-Noor is amusing.   You enter,
seat yourself at one of the numerous little tables set
out in a large room, and a tea-pot is immediately
placed before you, from which you are expected to
drink a deluge of hot tea before you may hope to
obtain anything in the shape of solid food.   After
you have done so, at the risk of swamping your
appetite, the Comptroller of the Table makes his
dignified appearance, entertaining you with an infini-
tude of small talk about things in general, and ends
by naming the various dishes to be had, your choice
of which is communicated to the Governor of the Pot.
Dinner is soon on table; but, if you wish to pass for
a well-bred man, do not venture to taste it until, rising
from your seat, you have invited everybody else in
the room to come and eat and drink with you.   Equal
good breeding compels them to refuse, and invite you
instead to do the same with them; the which, when
you have politely declined, you are at liberty to sit
down and eat your dinner in peace.

Getting into Tolon-Noor was difficult, getting out
of the wretched place equally so. It was a sort of
hop, skip, and jump with the poor camels; and their
driver, the servant with the long name, got into a

BELL AND IDOL FOUNDRY.

desperately bad temper with his difficulties; which,
however, he had self-control enough to manifest only
by perseveringly biting his lips. Oh, that all the ill-
tempered people in the world would confine themselves
to that expression of their feelings!

Fortunately, however, there was something better

than lips to be bitten. As they had had the luck to
bring a chicken with them, the fathers determined to
hold high festival upon it at their halting-place for the
night. For this purpose all set to work—M. Gabet
went to cut wood, their servant collected fuel in the
skirt of his coat, whilst M. Huc, installed as head-
cook, cut up and placed the fowl in their great cooking pot, with the appetizing addition of ginger-root
pickled in salt, onions, garlic, and spices. Samdadchiemba had been successful in his fuel-hunting, so
that the pot soon bubbled bravely. Withdrawn from
the fire, it was set upon the ground, and the three sat
round it, and with chop-sticks fished up their supper
from its recesses. They then went to rest with thankful hearts for this " table spread in the wilderness."

As they journeyed on in their westward course, a
dreadful storm of wind and rain brought them from
their previous fear of dying of thirst through want of
water, to that of dying of hunger, for fire was an im-
possibility, the wretched fuel of the desert being
soaked into mere pulp. In this distress, just as they
were about supping on oatmeal mixed with cold water,
two Tartars, leading a camel, came in sight, who
courteously addressed them: " Sirs, Lamas, this day
the heavens have fallen; you doubtless have been
unable to make a fire;" adding, " Men are all brothers,
and belong to each other, but laymen should honour
and serve the holy ones; therefore it is that we have
come to make a fire for you." Two good bundles of
fuel followed this kindly speech, a fire was kindled,
and hot oatmeal-porridge soon produced; which the
Tartars, to whom the feast was due, were invited to

share. Their welcome meal was taken cheerfully
together, and in the course of it an inquiry into the
military position of one of the Tartars brought out
the fact of his having been on duty at the time of the
war between the Chinese and the English—rebels of
the south, as they dubbed us—in 1840, though unfor-
tunately the strife was at an end before he had had an
opportunity of proving his valour upon these same
rebels.

It is pleasant sometimes to see things from another
point of view. At that period we English flattered
ourselves that we had beaten the Chinese, and, further,
compelled them to pay us for their own beating. At
their end of the world they have another version of
the story, which the Tartar proceeded to impart to his
amused friends. His account of the whole matter
was very simple : When the grand master, that is, the
Chinese Emperor, goes to war, he first sends forth his
own Chinese soldiers; and if these do not settle the business they of the *Solon* country are called out. If the
enemy is still obstinate enough to resist, then the aid of
the warriors of his, [the speaker's] country, is demanded,
the mere sound of whose march always compels them
to fly. So it was in the war with the rebels of the
south. First, the Chinese tried their hand, and did
nothing, spite of their having been told by their
superiors that if they only clashed their swords the
English "devils" [they are very polite to us !] would
run away. The next in order were summoned, but
equally in vain. Then came the Tartar contingent,
who furbished up their weapons with a will, though
informed by the discomfited Chinese (*Kitats* they call

SAVAGE REMOVING.

them) that they were marching to certain death, seeing
nothing could be done against sea-monsters, who lived
in the water like fish, came up to the surface when
least expected, for the purpose of discharging bomb-
shells at their opponents, and dived like frogs as soon
as a bow was bent at them.   Nothing daunted, the
Tartar forces still marched on—for six generations they
said they had received benefits from the sacred master
without being called on for any return, so it would
have been shame now to hang back—but the rebels
did not dare to meet them.   Hearing of their approach
they were seized with a panic, and implored peace;
which the sacred emperor mercifully granted them.

And this is a very neat little epitome of the Chinese
version of our war with them, as related to a couple
of Frenchmen by a retired Tartar shepherd-soldier.

Their new friends had helped them to a good meal;
but for bedding the travellers had to content themselves with furs water-sopped till they were more like
drowned cats than anything else, and the mere mud-
heap into which the rain had converted the tent-floor.
They felt doleful, but they were good men, and
thoughts of Him who had "not where to lay His
head" checked the rising discontent.

The route of our travellers, working their gradual
way south-west, now lay through some very character-
istic Tartar scenery, a sort of wild, grassy, everlasting
plain, unrelieved even by trees, but interrupted at
times by vast sheets of water, stately rivers, and rugged
mountains.   The monotony of these "limitless plains"
is occasionally broken by a richer pasture and abundant streams, which have attracted to them hordes of

this pastoral people, who camp in their midst until
their beasts have eaten up all the grass, when they
strike their tents and are off, bag and baggage, else-
where. These removals are picturesque sights to a
mere looker-on. The men and women, with their little
ones, are mounted on horses and oxen, upon which
also are packed their tents and few household goods:
the flocks and herds march by their side. The vehicle
on the right side of our little sketch of one of these
removals, is a Russian post-waggon, such as traverses
some of the wilds, thundering along with three horses
abreast.

Among these Tartars, the sole occupation of the
men is taking care of their flocks and herds, with an
occasional hunting expedition, not for sport, but for
food, when their bows and clumsy muskets come into
requisition. The training of their boys consists in
teaching them the use of bow and arrow and match-
lock, and to ride. This latter is accomplished by
setting the child on horseback behind a man, to whose
coat he has to cling with both hands to prevent being
jolted off, as the steed goes full gallop. By this process they become perfect horsemen, but in time get
so used to riding that they can scarcely walk, while
their legs are bowed by being constantly in the saddle.
A Tartar will even go to sleep on his camel rather
than be at the pains to dismount for his night's rest!

The women milk the cows, make butter and cheese,
go weary journeys to seek water—that being beneath
the dignity of their lords; collect fuel, dry and stack
it, and cook the food. They also full the cloth, tan
the hides, and then make them up into clothing,

which they embroider with great skill and taste.
These good dames will even construct serviceable,
if rather unshapely boots, both for themselves and
for their menkind, out of the leather which their own
hands have prepared.   Their dress consists of wide
trousers, with two upper garments, a long and a short
one, worn over them.   The head is protected by a
sort of bee-hive hat, painted red, and ornamented with
trinkets.   In-doors, the hair is divided into two long
tresses, which are ornamented with spangles of gold
and silver, pearls, and the like.   They are as much
at home on horseback as the men themselves.

The Tartar tent is composed of a wooden framework three feet high, surmounted by a number of
slanting poles, all meeting at the centre, where there
is a hole left to let out the smoke.   This skeleton tent
is covered with thick coarse linen.   The framework, it
should be said, is capable of being folded up.   The
entrance is so low that the visitor has to stoop his head
as he steps in over a beam of wood placed just in the
doorway.   The inside is divided into two apartments,
for the men and women separately.   Into the former
visitors are conducted; and he would be thought a very
ill-bred fellow who should venture into the ladies' side
of the house, where all the domestic utensils and
other properties are kept.   The fire-place, a mere
trivet, to hold the great family cooking-pot, is in the
centre of the tent.   Behind it, and facing the door,
is a singular piece of furniture, invariably found in
Tartar habitations, rich and poor alike; this is a kind
of shabby, faded small sofa, whose pillows have their
ends ornamented by plates of gilt and engraved

copper. This sofa is supposed to have special signi-
ficance, but what that is has not been discovered.
By it stands a square cupboard containing the family
ornaments: it is further utilized into an altar for

INTERIOR OF A TARTAR TENT.

their god Buddha, whose image, generally sitting, is
placed upon it, with nine copper vases, to receive the
daily offerings of milk, butter, water, and meal, ranged
before him. Prayer-books, wrapped in silk, are also
laid there; but woe to any layman who should venture to handle them ! none but a priest may do that.
Goats' horns, fixed in the wood-work of the tent, serve
for clothes pegs, meat hooks, and gun rests. The

prevailing aroma of this dwelling is that of ancient
mutton, grease, and butter: we need say no more
about it, or the uncleanly persons of its inmates.
The very highest magnates of the land are something
to shudder at in respect of cleanliness. Watch-dogs
bark around, but though you may need a stick to
fight your way through them, you must not on any
account enter the tent with it : that would be equivalent to intimating that its inmates were all dogs.
The stick being left outside, the visitor seats himself
by the master of the house, when pinches of snuff
and kind inquiries about the herds and flocks go
round.   The mistress of the family then, holding out
her hand to the guest, receives from him the wooden
cup that all Tartars carry about with them, and fills
it with tea, which is gratefully quaffed.   If well to
do in the world, the hostess adds butter, oatmeal,
cheese, or grated millet to the tea ; or possibly even
the distinguished attention of a bottle of warm Tartar
wine.   This is only skimmed milk, slightly fermented
and distilled ; poor, tasteless, washy stuff.

In one of these tents of the better sort our
travellers were entertained on a festival occasion.
Boiled mutton was the banquet; a whole sheep being
brought in, just cut into quarters.   The huge fat
tail—the fat alone of this will weigh from six to
eight pounds—was cut off and placed before the
strangers, as the dish of honour ; but they found it
so dreadful, that they were fain to get rid of it by
cutting it into little bits, and handing them to the
rest of the company, as an act of excessive politeness.
It was reluctantly taken.   "Too bad to deprive you

of it," was the animating spirit of those to whom it
was offered; but at last it was accepted, placed like the
rest of the food upon the knee (for there were no
plates), pulled to pieces with the fingers (for knives
there were none)—the fingers when too greasy being
wiped upon the jacket—and finally the tallowy mor-
sels were swallowed with great gusto, the Frenchmen
only too happy to get a slice out of the leg in exchange for the unpleasant lump which they had at
length got quit of. Singing to a rude three-stringed
violin followed, the performer being refreshed with
milk wine; and Timour, the Invincible, was the
burden of his song.

The Lamas are the only physicians these people
have. Their practice is to give vegetable remedies
only; but if drugs are not at hand, it is not of much
consequence, as the name of the one required, written
on a scrap of paper, rolled into a pill and swallowed,
does quite as well! They profess to see no difference
between swallowing the remedy itself and the mere
name of it. Prayers succeed the dose; for it is
imagined that illness is produced by some malignant
spirit who has got possession of the patient, and who
must be exorcised out of him. If the sufferer is
poor, a very short prayer is considered enough; if
very poor, the Lama physician contents himself with
prescribing patience. But if the patient is rich, a
very different process ensues. A whole college of
physicians will assemble in his tent, and give him
the benefit of a fortnight's prayers, accompanied perchance by a sort of cat's concert of noisy and brazen
musical instruments, whose din is reckoned service-

able in severe cases; nor will they stir from their post, until mutton and tea begin to fall short. If the patient recovers, their prayers have done it; if he dies, they have sent him to paradise, which is much better.

Once dead, the most favourite burial-place, for those who can afford it, is the Lamasery of the Five Towers; for thence the soul is certain to rise to some

LAMASERY OF THE FIVE TOWERS.

higher state of being. Indeed, one pious mourner there had the happiness of beholding the great Buddha himself—sitting cross-legged and doing nothing—by only applying his eye to a small hole in the mountain behind the Lamasery. Some of the Tartars will make a year's journey hither to lay the bones of their friends in this sacred soil; for which an immense sum is exacted. A Tartar king goes to his last rest magnificently. Gold and silver, precious stones, royal robes, and many slaves massacred for the purpose, are all buried with him; the mouth of the sepulchre being guarded by a curious machine, that has the power of shooting a number of arrows one after the other at any sacrilegious intruder.

The Lamaseries of Tartary are generally well built of brick and stone; for in what concerns their religious observances, the mild, simple people of that land are generous, and even lavish, in their gifts. If a temple to Buddha, with its Lamasery or college of priests, is to be erected, Lamas, duly accredited, go out over the whole kingdom to beg funds for the purpose. From tent to tent the sacred basin, which vouches for their commission, is carried and filled with offerings. The rich give ingots of gold and silver; from others, oxen, horses, and camels are accepted. And even the poor will not suffer themselves to be left out. Lumps of butter, furs, camel and horse hair ropes, are their offerings, and given apparently from their heart. Large sums are thus collected, and then the beautiful building rises fair amid the desert wastes of that dreary region.

Their style of architecture is peculiar and fanciful. Both inside and out they are covered with carvings of beasts, birds, and reptiles, the productions of the priests, who alone are permitted to have a hand in this part of the sacred work. The interior is also

decorated with paintings of wonderful richness of col-
ouring, and often of great truth to nature, save in the
matters of perspective and light and shade, of which,
truth to say, they have not the slightest notion.

BUDDHIST TEMPLE.

Opposite the principal entrance stands an altar upon
which an image of their god is placed, generally cross-
legged.   These figures are colossal, and have good

features, but are spoiled by the custom of making
their ears ridiculously long. In front of the idol
is a gilded seat for the chief Lama: divans surround the interior of the building, leaving just room
enough for the priests to move about in the course of
their duty. Bright shining copper vases are placed
before the idol, in which the people put their offerings
of milk, butter, wine, and meal; while numerous censers throw up a rich steam from aromatic plants, ever
burning there. Streamers, and lanterns of painted
paper and horn, hang hither and thither about the
temple.

The congregation is collected by successive blasts
on a conch shell; the chief Lama enters, seats himself on the altar, before which the ordinary Lamas,
having left their red boots at the entrance, pass in
respectful silence, throwing themselves almost upon
the ground before their chief, and then taking their
seats cross-legged on the divans. The rites begin by
a low murmured private prayer from each worshipper;
a brief silence, and a bell rings, which is succeeded
by a melodious chanted psalm, between whose parts
some coarse instruments of music perform a thundering interlude. The prayers are ordinarily in verse,
and well adapted to the musical form in which they
are used.

CHAPTER III.

S in what we familiarly call the East, so in
the wilds of Tartary, travellers form themselves into compact and numerous bodies,
called Caravans, for safety in their slow, long
journeys from land to land. In the course of their
route, our travellers fell in with one of these that
deserves a notice.

They were approaching a city called *Tchagan-
Kouren*—that means White Enclosure—one of the
finest, cleanest towns in the empire, which they had
been told would be reached in the course of the day;
but the sun was already set, and no city as yet in
sight. Advancing clouds of dust rising in the distance, at length took the shape of camels, laden with
goods for Pekin; and when the first camel-driver had
come up to them he was asked how far off Tchagan-
Kouren was. The man grinned as he answered
that the other end of the caravan was still in the
town. This was good news, as the missionaries concluded they had not far to go, when to their dismay
the man added that it was not more than three or

four miles off; his caravan, the other
end of which was still in it, comprising
at least ten thousand camels,—a statement enough to take away one's
breath.

These camel-drivers, clad from head
to foot in goat skins, and perched
lumpishly, like bales of goods, on

CARAVAN.

their animals, from whose necks sweet-toned bells

were suspended, seemed a stupid set; though before
they parted, riding past one and another in the interminable file, a word or two was occasionally got out
of them;—angry words at times, as the camels,
taking fright at Samdadchiemba's mule, broke their
ranks and gave their riders no small trouble to
get them right again. Wretched Sam.—the name is
really too long to write again so soon—enjoyed this
amazingly, and shouted with laughter, instead of
doing as his masters told him—keep himself and
his mule out of the way of the timid brutes. By
way of balancing the matter, mules and horses, it
is said, have a great objection to camels; so that
when regular inns were at length again met with, it
was occasionally somewhat troublesome to contrive
the stabling of the two together. The last of the ten
thousand was passed before the welcome town was
reached, and then the difficulty was to get a night's
lodging, every house being closed, and the streets
utterly deserted save by yelping curs, who, open-
mouthed, pursued the strangers. When at last some-
body was knocked up, no sooner were the camels
seen, than the door was briskly shut in their faces;
and this operation was repeated until it seemed as if
they must camp outside after all. Fortunately, when
they were nearly worn out, the owner of a mud-built
sheep-house perceived their distress, and courteously
addressing them as "Sirs, Lamas," bade them welcome, camels and all, to his poor dwelling. The good
man spread furs on the floor for his wearied guests,
from whence they were presently roused for an
appetizing supper of tea, cakes baked in the ashes,

and boiled mutton, set out on a stool that did duty for a table; and a hearty meal prefaced the welcome night's rest.

Their purpose was to cross the Hoang-ho, or Yellow River, otherwise "China's sorrow;" so called from its often overflowing its banks. This great river rises in the mountains of Thibet, and after traversing the empire north and south, east and west, with its magnificent waters, empties itself into the Yellow Sea, bringing down with it a vast quantity of mud. But the river was at this time in one of its overflowing conditions, widened into a sort of sea, whence rose, here and there, the tops of the higher lands; houses and villages also cropped up amid the flood, which, though gradually retiring, was yet sinking so slowly that it would be a whole month before the river was restored to its usual channel; and a month's lodging in an inn was precisely what the poor missionaries could not afford. Go on, therefore, they must, spite of the remonstrances of their hospitable host, at whom the sturdy muleteer laughed for his alarms, adding, that he supposed he himself tended his flocks with an umbrella in one hand, and a fan in the other.

The good old man, heedless of the mocker, saw them safely out of the town, and gave them parting dirctions for their course, which was toilsome enough, owing to the slimy mud left by the retiring inundation, through which the poor camels, trembling in every limb with fright, had to pick their way. The boatmen who had to ferry them over a lake, did their best to cheat the travellers, but did not succeed entirely to their mind, though they overcharged them considerably. The camels had to step their way over, the water being deep enough in some places to take them nearly up to the top of their humps; their long necks, of course, easily kept their heads above water. As these creatures cannot swim, the transit of them was an anxious thing to their masters.

The river was soon reached; but the boatmen at the ferry there were quite as clever as their brethren at the lake, in "taking in" their unfortunate clients. The preceding night was spent on their goat-skins, spread in the porch of an idol temple; one of the worshippers at which, in the course of his devotions, stole a handkerchief belonging to the party. A cruel cold night it was, and morning showed ice all around in the marshy soil. Cold was not all that had to be contended with. Camels will never, if they can help it, get into a boat. You may beat them to a mummy, if you are hard-hearted enough; you may jerk the bit in their poor noses to any extent your conscience will let you, but stir—into a boat—they will not. These two plans were tried, and tried in vain, until at length a bright idea for circumventing the obstinate beasts presented itself to the mind of one of the ferry-men, who instantly proceeded to put it in practice. He made so sudden and violent a tilt, with his whole strength, at the hinder end of one of the camels, as threw it forward, so that, to avoid tumbling on its nose, it was obliged to place its fore feet in the boat, close to which it was placed before the manœuvre was executed. One half of it in, the other half was easily induced to follow. A second camel was got aboard in the same manner. The creatures were, however,

ENTRANCE TO THE HONG-KONG.

aware that they had been overreached in the transaction, and, contrary to their usual amiability, they expressed their displeasure pretty strongly whenever the offending boatman came near them in the course of their transit.

It was wretchedly marshy travel when they got to the other side; and upon approaching the Little River, which had to be crossed after its wide-flowing yellow brother, they determined on pitching their tent for a few days' rest before proceeding.

Rest was needful, not only to repair the fatigues of the past, but for the purpose of holding a grand washing-day for their clothes, which they had been compelled to wear unchanged for six weeks. That would have been a trifle to a Tartar, or Chinese, but to educated Europeans it was downright distressing; and great was their rejoicing when, after soaking the things in a pond, and beating them on a stone, they at length folded them up thoroughly clean.

During their "rest and be thankful" on the bank of the Little River, the day's work was portioned out as follows:—By dawn they rose, rolled up their goat-skin beds, which were put out of the way in a corner, swept out their tent, placed the cooking things in order, washed their wooden cups-of-all-work, polished the kettle, and cleaned their clothes, all to the admiration of the Tartars who visited them, and who could not altogether understand such fastidious doings. Prayers followed, and then a quiet, meditative stroll in the desert, occupied with pious meditations, from pious and grateful hearts. The next business was to collect fuel for a fire, to cook breakfast, consist-

ing of tea, and cakes baked in the ashes, the grain
for which had first to be pounded into flour; mill,
of course, they had none.   Breakfast despatched, the
servant with the five-syllabled name—quite too long
for every-day use—gave his attention to the beasts,
while his masters again betook themselves to prayer.
A little nap at noon followed, for they sat up late at
night to enjoy its various beauties.   Then was the
time for all the noisy-tongued water-fowl to come
forth, and fill the moonlight air with their pleasant
clamour; wild ducks and geese, teal, storks, and
bustards, on their annual visit to the country.   One
little beast of a bird, called by the Chinese, Dragon's
Foot, was a very dragon in temper, bristling up even
the hairs on its legs if one offered to touch it, and
pecking fiercely at the hand that ventured to caress
it, when it was caught.   It was not bad to eat, only
intolerably tough.

The Tartars do not care to make food of this wealth
of eatable birds that is annually brought to their
hungry plains.   Fat mutton, half boiled, is their
principal delicacy; nor do they vary it by the fish
with which their lakes and ponds teem.   The Chinese
know better, and are kind enough to fish the Tartar
lakes for their stupid owners.   Near to the travellers'
camping-place one of their fishing-stations afforded
them an opportunity of seeing how the Chinese, in
those parts, go a-fishing.   At night, gliding about in
their boats on the tranquil water, the fishermen keep
up a continual beating of wooden drums to frighten
the fish into the nets already laid for them; and one
fellow, who was resting himself over his tea, engaged

to take the missionaries with him, in order to show them what, with the usual Chinese polite self-depreciation, he called his "unskilful and disagreeable"

FISHING PARTY.

fishing. The boat sped through troops of water-fowl to the spot where the nets, floated by pieces of wood, were glittering with fish, the largest only of which were captured, those weighing less than half a pound being turned into the water again. It was a successful night's work; but when the fisherman proposed to sell some of his fine produce to the two, they were obliged to own that they could not afford to buy it. So the matter ended by his frankly making them a present of the little fish, which were too small to sell; a gift that rejoiced the heart of the camel-driver, as well as their own, for it was a pleasant variety from their everlasting oatmeal and tea, with occasional mutton. These small, despised fish, turned out excellent in the eating.

The passage of the Little River was at last effected with considerable difficulty, though aided by the gratitude of a poor fisherman, whose injured leg the travellers had dressed; to his great astonishment not only not demanding anything for the service rendered, but absolutely refusing recompense. It was sad struggling through the mud, and night fell before they could set up their tent on dry ground, and lie down to rest, after a sumptuous supper of cold water and a few handfuls of millet. Prayer, as usual, sweetened the hardship to these good men, and they slept peacefully in their poor lodging.

A dreary desert, called that of Ortous, received them when progress was resumed. A miserable, sandy, rocky, waterless plain it was; such pasture as occasionally cropped up in it, being so deep down in the sand, that the beasts had to grub it up with their noses in the earth. Cultivation was here struggling with wild, uncultivated life, both of inhabitants and soil; the labourers being a mixed population, half Chinese, half Tartars, possessing the bad qualities of each. Hemp is the principal agricultural produce, after the little grain crop that supplies their scanty living. The mode of getting in the hemp is slovenly, so that the stumps left standing in the fields were a sore impediment to the camels, who went stumbling over them. There were advantages, however, attending this bad farming—it is said all evils have their corresponding good—the woody stumps furnishing excellent fuel when the travellers camped for the night. But the want of water, distressing as it was to the men of the party, who were glad to get a bucket or two of muddy, brackish stuff whenever they were fortunate enough to meet with it, was much worse to their beasts, who evidently drooped under the unwonted privation. It was a wretched country, and poor as were the travellers themselves, their humanity yet led them to give, of their poverty, to the still poorer inhabitants of that wretched district, who overwhelmed them with all manner of high-sounding titles as persuasives to alms-giving. A few leaves of tea, a little millet, or oatmeal, and some mutton fat were all they had to give, but it was thankfully received. As the Tartars are wandering tribes, their remaining in such bad quarters may occasion some surprise; but in truth, wanderers though they are, their wanderings are limited to their own district, as a species of slavery, or rather serfage, exists among them in full force—a slavery which, though it ties them to the soil, is mild enough, so far as the relation between the so-called slave and his master is concerned. The Tartar name for slave is, in truth, brother; but, as will always be the case, the relationship is at times abused by the master. An ingenious mode of oppressing slaves, as practised by one chief, is to give a number of his worst cattle, camels, sheep, goats, into their care, and in a few years demanding the return of them, when he takes care to require, in their place, healthy, stalwart beasts, possibly to a much larger amount than the original herds, and this on the pretence that in that time his cattle must have multiplied.

The various Tartar lords, or monarchs, all acknowledge the sovereignty of the Emperor of China.

Wading their way through the sands of the Ortous, the missionaries were one day accosted by a Lama, who courteously reproached them with passing his Lamasery without stopping to render their adoration to the presiding saint. He was told that those whom he addressed worshipped only the Lord Jehovah, creator of heaven and earth; no mere man was entitled to their worship. The Lama replied, that the saint he wished them to stop and worship was an incarnation of Buddha himself; a child seven years old, for whom they had in haste constructed a Lamasery. But finding the Christians still obdurate, he turned bridle, and rode off in something of a pet.

These superior Lamas, or human representatives of their god—living Buddhas they are called—assume their position in some such way as the following:— The worshippers of Buddha, it should be said, believe in what is called the transmigration of souls; that is, that when any creature—man or beast—dies, its soul immediately goes into another body. When, therefore, one of these Lamas dies, it is taken for granted he will make his appearance upon earth again in another body, most likely that of a child. Certain circumstances are supposed to point out the favoured little one, and painful, and even perilous, pilgrimages are undertaken to the spot,

generally in some exceedingly out-of-the-way place in
Thibet, where he is to be found. But before he is
acknowledged as a living Buddha, a prescribed form
has to be gone through. He is presented to an
assembly of priests, who put various questions to him
in order to satisfy themselves of his identity with the
dead Lama. The poor child is, of course, tutored
to answer these questions in the desired manner, and
to point out, among the various articles presented to
him for the purpose, the prayer-books, tea-cups, and
the like, that he was wont to use in his former life
on earth. The examination successfully concluded,
he is hailed as their spiritual head, and carried off in
triumph to the Lamasery of which he is to be the
superior; and where, as well as on his journey to it,
he receives the adoration and offerings of his miserable, deluded worshippers.

The life which this young living Buddha is condemned to live is not very exhilarating, if we may
judge from one specimen of it, with whom the party
fell in, in the desert, and who became their companion for awhile. He was a fine gentlemanly young
fellow of eighteen, and seemed sorely put out by
his dignity, which effectually prevented his enjoying
himself, as his frank, lively nature would have led
him to do. Young, strong, and active, instead of
dashing about on his steed, as he would have liked,
there sat he solemnly between two horsemen, who
never left him for a minute. When they camped,
and a little diversion after his long, stiff ride, would
have been agreeable, he was doomed to squat on a
cushion in a corner, like a make-believe idol. The

only recreation the poor lad got, was an occasional
chat with the Frenchmen in their tent, where he
could lay aside his cumbrous godship, and enjoy
himself like an ordinary mortal.   He was wont to

ELECTION OF A LIVING BUDDHA.

inquire with an appearance of interest into their
doctrines, which he commended; but resisted all
attempts to draw him out on the subject of his supposed previous transmigrations, saying that it gave
him pain.   Doubtless he knew it was vain to delude
them with the lies that imposed upon his worshippers.

Beside the living Buddha, or Superior Lama, who
is an object of worship, there is in each Tartar district

or kingdom another Superior Lama, of royal birth, for business matters ; and he governs the college or Lamasery.   The members of it are divided, as in colleges nearer home, into masters, or tutors, and students.   The student is the master's " fag," lighting his fire, sweeping his room, and rendering to him those other little menial offices which are familiar enough at our own public schools.   In coincidence also with the traditions of these institutions at home, the scholar is occasionally soundly beaten, when he has not done his lessons ; and the impression on his mind (as we understand it is in some instances with ourselves) is, that a good flogging contributes sensibly to his improvement in learning.

A few days' further journey in this wild, bleak country, made the travellers acquainted with the sudden changes of temperature which add to the distress of the austere climate of Tartary. Though it was but autumn, the cold of winter suddenly fell upon them.   A large fire was lighted in the tent, in addition to which they threw over their shivering frames the large sheep-skin robes which they had bought in the earlier stage of the expedition.   But the fuel was green, and its acrid, blinding smoke, was intolerable to their European eyes, from which it drew copious tears, as they huddled themselves into a miserable heap to escape it.   Their merciless servant, accustomed to this Tartar torment, laughed at them amain, and had even life enough left in him to crack jokes upon his " spiritual fathers," whose " large, bright eyes," were nearly put out by the smoke, while his little, ugly ones, as he frankly termed them, were none the worse for such wear. The night was passed in sufficient discomfort; and though at noon next day the atmosphere was milder, the stream near which they had camped remained so hard frozen that the camels, to assuage their thirst, were found licking the ice, which the horse and mule, with their better armed feet, were stamping on, in a vain attempt to break. A few strokes of the hatchet relieved the poor creatures, by opening a way to the water beneath. They had two days of this extreme cold; so extreme that the tent pegs were frozen into the ground, requiring repeated applications of boiling water to enable them to be withdrawn. The first extracted without this process snapped like glass. Yet when the missionaries took their departure, the weather had become so mild again that they were glad to doff their sheep-skin coats, and pack them up out of the way.

Their westward course brought them in contact with numerous caravans of pilgrims proceeding to a Lamasery at a place called Rache-Tchurin, where one of the most extraordinary ceremonies connected with Buddhic religious faith was to take place. This extraordinary and very disagreeable ceremony is, that one of the Lamas cuts himself open, in the sight of the congregation, and then comes all right again, none the worse for his misadventure. It is not every priest who possesses power to perform this juggling trick, for such it must be; and the more sober-minded Lamas repudiate it altogether. But with the vulgar it takes amazingly, and a sufficient supply of Boktès —that is the name of the performers—is therefore

always to be found.   Lamas of inferior skill content
themselves with licking red-hot iron without burning
their tongues, gashing their bodies without leaving
any mark, and other such conjurers' exhibitions.

BARBAROUS LAMANESQUE CEREMONY.

The good missionaries longed to proceed to the
scene of this vile delusion, and there testify of the
true God in the very teeth of the false one and his
disgusting service ; but their determination to do so
was prevented by the circumstance of the little
caravan losing itself in the desert, after the Abbé
Gabet had left them to buy provisions.   A meeting-
place had been arranged, to which he was to repair
when he had done his marketing ; but when he and

his camel arrived at the spot, not a creature was to be seen! He looked hither and thither in vain, asked vain questions when other travellers came in sight—for seeking lost companions in a Tartar desert is like seeking a needle in a bottle of hay—and at last had to give it up in despair, camping for the night solitary and supperless. His friends, meanwhile, were in no less distress about him. They had lost their way amid the fine, wave-like sand of the desert, and, aided by Samdadchiemba's obstinacy—who insisted that they were quite right, he knew all about travelling—came to grief, and a complete stand-still at night. Camping was inevitable; so the tent was got up, one camel tethered, and the muleteer despatched on the other to hunt up the missing " elder spiritual father." But the tethered beast, not liking solitude, soon managed to break its cord, and was off, no one knew whither; the horse and mule followed for company, and M. Huc was left in a tolerably awkward predicament.

The horse and mule were found next day, by the forlorn missionary; not so his brother Gabet, who, in the hue and cry raised after him, was described to passers-by as a tall Lama, with a red face, long nose, and large gray beard, and moreover habited in yellow and red. This fascinating description did not do much; but at length the missing man " turned up " of himself, and after a good laugh over their tribulations, now that they were at an end, the route towards the Lamasery was resumed. The Abbé had thought it right to deliver a lecture to his servant on that wilfulness of his which had brought them into such

distress ; to which the gentle youth made no reply at
the time.   But when it came to saddling the camels,
there sat he doggedly on a stone, without offering to
stir.   In answer to the reprimand of his masters on
this score, he coolly told them that if they wished to
set out they might do so ; as for himself, he intended
to remain where he was—what possible use could they
have for such a one as the Abbé, in the course of
his scolding, had made him out to be.   His masters
knew he was a strange being, so they took no notice
of his petulance, quietly doing his work themselves,
whilst he watched them through his fingers.   Seeing
they got on perfectly well without him, my lord
thought it was not worth while to hold out.   Up he
rose, saddled and mounted his mule, and led the way
as usual, but in silence ; his good-natured masters
smiling at each other about his nonsense, though they
did not care to vex him further by noticing it.   Their
evening meal of sheep's liver and flour, in the procur-
ing of which Gabet had lost his companions, removed
the cloud from Master Samdadchiemba's face, and he
applied himself with unusual zeal to the cooking of
their festive entertainment.

Morning brought them in sight of the Lamasery
of which they had been in quest.   Three temples
formed its centre, surrounded by numerous white
huts.   The quiet streets showed only red-scarfed
Lamas, who whispered out the proper salutation, and
then continued their stroll.   In one street was seen
a young Lama in the performance of a singular act
of devotion—that of going round the Lamasery,
measuring the ground with his length at every step !

His forehead touched the earth at each measurement, while his hands and arms were first placed in the attitude of prayer, and then used to draw a line with a goat's horn, carried for the purpose, on each side his prostrate body. Instead of going the round of the sacred buildings in this manner, some perform it beneath a staggering load of prayer-books, all the contents of which they are in consequence supposed to have recited. Others make the circuit telling beads, or carrying a prayer-machine—a little wheel turned by hand—whose rapid revolutions are supposed to send off supplications to heaven, for the benefit of the grinder. In some of the monasteries, barrels, inscribed with favourite prayers, are placed on an axis, and spun round for the behoof of such as are too idle to measure their length round the temple, or to carry donkey-loads of books. As long as the barrel revolves, which it will do for some time after it is put in motion, its revolutions count for prayers to him who has set it a-going, and who may meantime eat, drink, and sleep as he pleases, without interfering with its efficacy. Two Lamas were found on the point of fighting over a prayer-barrel which one had set turning on his own account, and the other had stopped, and then set off for himself, as soon as the back of the first comer was turned. They kept up their contest for some time, one spinning, the other stopping it, and *vice versa*, until at length an aged priest healed the quarrel by himself taking charge of the machine, and turning it for the benefit of both.

CHAPTER IV.

THE further course of our friends across the dreary Ortous country brought into view one morning a large caravan, which was seen advancing through a defile between two lofty mountains. It was a very large one: camels, horses, with their richly-dressed riders, all betokened the approach of some important personage. Presently up dashed four cavaliers, who formed a sort of vanguard to the troop behind them. The blue button on their caps showed them to be mandarins; and they addressed a courteous greeting to the travellers, asking them whence they were, and whither going. Their curiosity on this point being satisfied, the same questions were put to them in return, when it was answered that they were conducting one of the Tartar chiefs, or kings, tributary to China, on his annual visit to his imperial master at Pekin—it being imposed upon all the subject princes to present themselves yearly at a certain time before the Emperor, and do him homage.

Behind the mandarins came the palanquin of the monarch. It was a square, slightly-ornamented vehicle, borne by two mules, the one before, the other

behind; the first mule was led by a white-bearded
Lama, excellently mounted, whose presence in this
office was supposed to insure safety for the whole
expedition. The occupant of the palanquin, a good-
humoured-looking plump man of fifty, squatted cross-
legged within it; and he replied to the missionaries'
salute by a cordial expression of good wishes for the
"men of prayer." In the rear of the palanquin, a
remarkably beautiful white camel, whose humps were
decorated by streamers of yellow silk, was led by
a silken cord, as a present for the sacred master.
Around the carriage a guard of horsemen pranced,
and executed a variety of such manœuvres as became
the centaur-like riders of the desert. Baggage-
camels completed the procession.

The last of the pageant had long disappeared when
the tent was pitched for the night. As tea was
being made, three mandarins, two of whom wore
respectively the red and the blue button, rode up to
the travellers to ask news of the caravan, from which
they had been separated, and on hearing of its distance,
at once invited themselves to spend the night with
their new friends. They unsaddled their horses, and
sent them off into the desert to take care of themselves, as they sat down by the fire. One of these
guests, he with the red button, proved to be the chief
minister of the king they had met in the early part
of the day, and was a clever, well-bred man. This
gentleman informed his hosts that all the monarchs
of the world—by which he meant his own part of it
—went to Pekin every three years to celebrate the
new year; those who, like his own master, lived

comparatively near the capital, attended there every
year: on which occasions the sovereigns were permitted to prostrate themselves before the old Buddha
—that is, the Emperor; a felicity accorded to themselves alone, as it was strictly denied to their
followers.   The tribute demanded of them under the
name of offerings, was conveyed to the Emperor at
this time.   It consists of camels, fine horses, and
Tartar produce of various kinds—deer, bear, and
goats' meat, pheasants, mushrooms, fragrant plants,
all frozen.   Pheasants' eggs are the peculiar tribute
of one department of the empire, demanded for the
special purpose of beautifying the hair of the ladies
of the imperial household.   The lower classes have
the pleasure of furnishing beasts for the transport of
these articles to the court; and as the journey takes
place in the dead of winter, the duty is a harassing
and costly one, many of the poor animals dying on
the way through scarcity of food.

When the tributary kings arrive at Pekin, they
are lodged, with their attendants, each one in a house
specially prepared for him, and the whole is placed
under the charge of a high mandarin.   As there are
sometimes two hundred of these kings so called, it
is rather busy work to provide for them, and keep
everybody in order.

New Year's Day is the grand day of the festival.
The Emperor then visits in state what is known as
the temple of his ancestors, to render homage to
their memory.   A long avenue leading to this temple
is lined on both sides by the two hundred tributaries,
in magnificent silken robes embroidered with gold

and silver. When the Emperor leaves his palace, not
a soul among his subjects must be seen in the streets;
death would be the punishment of such audacity.
Heralds proclaim the approach of the "Lord of the.

GRAND CEREMONY AT THE ANCESTRAL TEMPLE.

Earth," to whom the two hundred offer "ten thousand congratulations," and then drop on their faces
before him, who marches through their prostrate
ranks to the temple, pays his devotions there, and
returns again between the two rows of princes, still
with their noses in the very dust before him. After
this they are permitted to rise, and repair to the

habitations assigned to them, rejoicing, if they have
had good luck, at having had the happiness of beholding the yellow robe of their master. To see
more is out of the question, as to raise the head while
thus grovelling before the Emperor would be dealt
with as a heinous crime.

Of course these tributary kings receive gifts in
return for their own. During the war with the
English, the Emperor, being short of cash, was ingenious enough to pay his tributaries in ingots of
copper, gilt, instead of the accustomed golden ones.
Not a word was said by the recipients; they were
obliged to pocket the affront, as it would never have
done to intimate, however delicately, that his majesty
had been "passing" false coin.

From information supplied by their Tartar friends
before they galloped off at daybreak, the missionaries
were induced to somewhat alter the route which they·
had purposed following on their long journey to the
end of the world, as the Chinese are pleased to call'
Thibet: beyond it, they hold, there is only shoreless
sea. The new route led them to re-cross the Yellow
River, and travel through the Chinese province of
Kan-Sou, to the Tartar tribes of the Koukou-Noor.
Formerly it would have been a perilous thing for
them to enter China; but, regularly Tartarized as
they were by hard travel, and familiar as they had
become with Chinese manners and ordinary speech,
they had no scruples about venturing. Samdadchiemba decidedly approved of the change, as good
tea was to be had there, and better shelter than the
deserts had afforded.

In accordance with this change of plan, the route, which had hitherto been westward, was caused to diverge slightly towards the south; and a few hours' travel made them glad to stop and dine on half-baked doughy bread and brackish water. A Tartar, who joined them at this delicate refreshment, and sniffed thrice at their empty snuff-box by way of dessert, gave them some directions for their journey, including the whereabouts of a well of detestable water—detestable, as he averred, by reason of a demon having corrupted it. This was not very encouraging, but it could not be helped; so on they went until the demon-possessed well came in view, and there they prepared to pass the night.

The Tartar had done no injustice to this well. Their servant was sent to draw from it, and returned with a basin full of dirty, muddy, ill-smelling water, on whose surface floated some greasy abomination—sight and smell were quite enough without tasting it. Fortunately the missionaries had some knowledge of chemistry. A little wood was found, and burned into charcoal, which, broken small, was put into a boiling kettle-ful of the odious fluid. Their Tartar servant, who was not a chemist, sat staring by, wondering what sort of soup was to be made of burnt wood and dirty water. Presently it was poured out and filtered, —nothing to boast of, certainly, but still drinkable; and an ocean of tea was brewed with it, in which a pinch of oatmeal was mixed by way of rendering it meat as well as drink. Samdadchiemba was in a paroxysm of wonderment about the affair, protesting that his own Lamas, who pretended to know everything, would have died of thirst before they had found out how to make such stuff fit for use. And then, seeing the purifying properties of charcoal, he asked whether rubbing his face with it would make it as white as his masters';—a question no sooner asked than laughed at by himself, looking at his own black hands which had broken up the charcoal.

Two days' journey brought them to the foot of lofty, cloud-topped mountains, which had to be scaled with painful toil both to man and beasts, the feet of the poor camels bleeding with the ruggedness of the ascent. The crest gained, showed at their base the Yellow River rolling its majestic current from south to north, and nightfall brought the travellers to its banks. The passage of the stream was more successful than on the former occasion: the ferrymen were less exacting, the camels less contrary, but—there always is a but—their dog had to be left behind, the boatmen insisting that dogs ought to be able to swim across, and not take up the room of their betters in the boat—an opinion in which we entirely coincide. They disembarked in China, leaving the desert and wandering life for a time behind them.

CHAPTER V.

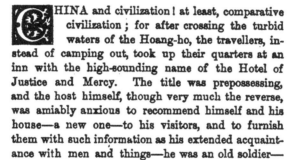HINA and civilization! at least, comparative civilization; for after crossing the turbid waters of the Hoang-ho, the travellers, instead of camping out, took up their quarters at an inn with the high-sounding name of the Hotel of Justice and Mercy. The title was prepossessing, and the host himself, though very much the reverse, was amiably anxious to recommend himself and his house—a new one—to his visitors, and to furnish them with such information as his extended acquaintance with men and things—he was an old soldier—had acquired for him.

Provisions in this little Chinese town were both abundant and good; and they were to be got easily, which is more than can be said of some places nearer home. All manner of food, cooked and ready for the eating, was at all hours of the day to be had, and brought home to the traveller, at varying prices to suit both rich and poor. Some such plan as that adopted at Ché-Tsui-Dze, would be amazingly useful to solitary people in London.

Two days were spent comfortably here before resuming their progress towards the goal of their

enterprise, and stronghold of Buddhism, Lha-Ssa in
Thibet.

Once more on the road, an hour's time brought
them to the Great Wall of China, or rather, the
ruinous portion of it at that point. This celebrated
wall was erected about two hundred years before
Christ, to check the incursions of the Mantchou
Tartars, who subsequently gave a long line of
sovereigns to China. It was composed of earth,
cased with strong masonry on each side to support
it, and having brick-work on the top. It was twenty-
five feet high, and twenty-five broad at the base,
sloping upwards to a surface of fifteen feet. Its
length is about fifteen hundred miles, over hill and
over dale; and, originally, at about every hundred
yards was a kind of fort, or guard-house, thirty-seven
feet high, and forty feet square at the base. In some
parts of the country this wonderful wall still retains
its architectural and military character; in others it
is merely a heap of flint stones roughly put together.

The country in this neighbourhood was pleasing,
and bore marks of one of the principal virtues of the
Chinese—their great industry. "Gather up the
fragments, that nothing may be lost," is a divine
injunction more completely obeyed and carried out
in China than in any Christian country, though with
our recent chemical discoveries we are now following
hard after the example there set us. The odds and
ends that are turned to account with the overabound-
ing population of that empire, is something mar-
vellous.

The Chinese plan for watering the ground for

GREAT WALL OF CHINA.

agricultural purposes, is, as seen in this district of Kan-Sou, admirable. Channels cut in the banks of the Hoang-ho convey its waters first into broad reservoirs : these afterwards pour their contents into others, whence the ditches that surround the fields are supplied. Well contrived, yet simple machinery, raises the water from its source, and distributes it over the land in an orderly, regular manner, furnishing each farmer in his turn with the life-giving stream, which, in the watering season, so overspreads the land, that small boats carry the owners over their own fields; or perchance they get along in buffalo carts with immensely high wheels. These arrangements for irrigation are kept in order by official inspection. A mandarin engaged in this duty was met by our travellers, whom he greeted courteously, spite of the kicking and curveting of his horse, to whom their camels were an abomination. Camels were inevitable to the party, but from time to time got them into trouble. The inhabitants here have few villages ; they live chiefly in separate farms surrounded by corn-fields, the ripened grain of which is stacked on the flat roofs of the houses.

The little party traversed the province of Kan-Sou with various fortune; lodging now in small but convenient inns, where food was both good and cheap; now in a military guard-house, which, in its frequent occurrence on the great roads, has rude accommodation for travellers; and at length arrived at a large village, where they put up at the Hotel of the Five Felicities. The Chinese are much more ingenious in naming their hotels than we are. While attending

to their beasts here, up rode a horseman with a white
button in his cap, who shouted to the landlord to
send off the Tartars and their camels immediately, as

IRRIGATION OF THE FIELDS.

his master, a great mandarin, was coming to lodge in
his house, and would not have camels about it. The
poor inn-keeper, seeing his Tartar guests took no notice
of this speech, respectfully begged them to take
themselves away; and was told in reply, and in
hearing of the insolent White Button, that as the
travellers had been received in the inn, there they

would stay—no mandarin should drive them out.
And the messenger himself was reminded that, as the
servant of a great mandarin, and decorated with a
white button to boot, he was bound to be not only
polite, but just.   White Button did not much like
this, but as there was no help for it he rode back to his
master, and presently returned, saying, courteously,
that as they were all brothers they were bound to
accommodate each other, each giving way a little,
and so manage the difference.   There was no gain-
saying such sound doctrine, so the camels were tied
up where they were least likely to frighten the great
man's horses, and by the time he arrived everything
was comfortably arranged : there was room enough
in the world for both.   But in this apparently insig-
nificant matter the missionaries felt they had gained
a point, seeing it was at the peril of their lives that
they had entered the country ; for such indeed was
the law of China.

The little village of Ever-flowing Waters, which
received them one night, was a delightful-looking
rest-place, worthy of its poetical name, with its
rivulet-traversed streets, cheerful stone houses painted
white or red, and its beautiful trees.   It was a lovely
village, but the excessively high charges inflicted upon them by their host were a decided drawback on
the pleasant impression which it made.   How very
like home experiences this is !

Further on, at the Hotel of the Three Social Rela-
tions, the landlord, a good-humoured, fussy Chinese,
asked the travellers whether they were not English;
adding, to render himself quite intelligible, that by

English he meant the sea-devils who were making war at Canton. He was answered that his guests were not devils of any kind, either sea or land; upon which a by-stander promptly interposed, telling him he knew nothing of physiognomy, for the sea-devils had all blue eyes and red hair, which the travellers had not. This indisputable truth settled the matter; the host further remarking that the sea-devils, otherwise English, never ventured to quit the sea, as when on dry land they died off like fish out of water.

The missionaries, now arrived at the junction of the Chinese province Kan-Sou and the Tartar country of Koukou-Noor, found it needful to make up their minds as to the remainder of their journey; whether to push on to the Thibetian capital of Lha-Ssa, notwithstanding the difficulties of the way, or give up the perilous undertaking entirely. Four months' travelling had already been passed, not in the easiest manner possible; and that which lay before them was represented to them in the most deterring manner. Robbers, cold of winter, heat of summer, deserts, all were pressed into the service to frighten them out of their plan; but finding that caravans of merchants from time to time followed the route, they determined not to have less courage in prosecuting their sacred mission than these traffickers displayed in pursuit of gain.

A small caravan of Khalkha Tartars, on their journey from the frontiers of Russia to Lha-Ssa, to pay their homage to a new Lama, seemed to offer facilities for our travellers' getting there. They were men of rank, and well armed, including the possession

of a very small cannon, mounted between the humps
of a camel, after the manner of the Chinese. But
as they proposed galloping the entire distance, accompanying them was out of the question; so the

KHALKHA TARTARS.

missionaries reluctantly resigned themselves to waiting
for more suitable company, resolving to employ their
detention in studying the language and religion of
the country they intended to visit. The Abbé Gabet
was therefore despatched to a celebrated Lamasery,

that of Kounboum, to seek a teacher, and soon returned with one, who appeared everything they could desire. Learned and agreeable, Sandara the Bearded —so called on account of the size of his beard—soon professed great interest in the religion of his pupils, inquired thoughtfully about its doctrines, repeated their prayers, and performed other devotional offices, in so devout and heartfelt a manner as to gladden the very souls of his amiable employers, as they ventured to believe him a true disciple of their Lord. Alas! Sandara with the beard was simply an accomplished hypocrite, and soon threw off the disguise he had assumed. The change was astounding; he could not even behave decently to his clerical friends while engaged in instructing them. Sometimes he would jeer at them for their stupidity in requiring a second explanation of some lesson already given, remarking to them that even a donkey would remember what had been told him three times over. Altogether he made himself a complete pest; yet, domestic perpetual blister as he was, they decided on retaining him in his post of tutor, for he was really clever, and they felt that their progress under his rude teaching would be the surer, as their faults and blunders were rebuked with an emphasis that rendered forgetfulness impossible. Ill-temper, however, was not his only fault; for, in addition to other small knaveries, he meanly endeavoured to shake their confidence in the honesty of their faithful servant, who, uncouth and self-willed as he was, had still the merit of being genuine in his dealings.

Their host in this town was a Mohammedan, of

whom there are many in China, where they hold their own with the best of the disciples of Confucius, not slinking about, oppressed and miserable, like the Christians. The reason of this, according to the

CONFUCIUS, THE GREAT MORAL TEACHER OF THE CHINESE.

Abbé Huc, is that they stand boldly one by another, and by their united action compel the Government to respect them. They are distinguished by wearing a blue cap: rather a needful precaution, as their countenances have gradually acquired the true Chinese type—prominent cheek-bones, flat noses, and sunken eyes.

The first day of the New Year, a festival in China as almost everywhere, was now at hand, and all was hurry and bustle to prepare for it. In this country, as in more civilized ones, there is one especial annoyance of the season—that of paying your debts and making others pay you. Out rushes John Chinaman into his neighbour's house, clamouring for his due, and then comes back to find his own turned upside down by an impatient creditor. The confusion and worry culminate on the last day of the year, when the whole town is in an uproar; people running to and fro, staggering under burdens of clothes, beds, cooking-vessels, anything, in short, either of their own or their neighbours, borrowed under pretence of being returned immediately, upon which they can raise a trifle at the pawnbroker's, to satisfy the urgent demands which, by that time, *must* be satisfied. Twelve o'clock at night puts an instantaneous stop to this: no more demanding or paying of debts; the most irate suddenly become amiable, and he who was just on the point of wringing his neighbour's neck, now clasps it lovingly in his arms.

The observance of the day is much after our own fashion. Fine clothes, dinner-parties, presents, visits, theatres, fireworks, and other amusements, fill up its hours; and, as at home, the excitement is kept up for several days. After these, business is resumed; except by such as wish to declare themselves bankrupt—a condition which, in the Chinese speech, is expressed by "leaving the door open." The Mohammedans in China do not keep their New Year at the same time with their neighbours, so that in their own lodging the missionaries had a quiet time of it, which they spent in studying their Thibetian lessons

so far into the night as led their sharp-eyed landlord
in the first place to put the oil-bottle out of their
reach, and in the second to charge his inmates extra
for light; a measure which in that happy land is, it
appears, reckoned exceptional and exceptionable.
The good man doubtless thought himself clever; but
as the priests were clever also, they bought a parcel
of candles, for which they constructed a candlestick
out of half a carrot and a long nail.

Their lodging here was but temporary, and at the
suggestion of Sandara the Bearded, it was determined
that whilst awaiting the caravan to Thibet, their
residence should be in his own Lamasery of Kounboum, for the purpose of study.   Preparations for
departure were accordingly made, somewhat retarded
by the circumstance of their tent, which had been
lent to the landlord for a pic-nic, having to be
reclaimed from the pawn-shop, whither he had
conveyed it for his own benefit! Its extraction from
this bourne—whence travellers do not always return—
was due primarily to Sandara, who thumped the table
till the teacups danced again, by way of enforcing
his demand for the missing property, which was re-
deemed by a miscellaneous collection of household
furniture, hastily caught up and pledged in its
stead.

It was dead winter, so that when the little cavalcade
started next day, with the tent triumphantly packed
on a cart, it presently met with a mishap: in crossing
a small stream, on the ice, down tumbled the vehicle
in a heap of ruin; but with the help of a big stone,
some pieces of stick, and rope ends, it was cleverly

ACCIDENT ON THE RAILROAD

patched up again by their Chinese driver; the Chinese
being the handiest fellows in the world.

The Lamasery was reached in the dark; but under
a clear sky, and with countless stars of unwonted
brilliance, the white buildings, together with the fan-
tastic outline of the temple itself, were plainly
discernible as they passed along the utterly silent
streets. Sandara found them a lodging for the night,
as also a good supper of tea, with milk, mutton,
butter, and excellent bread. This was succeeded in
the morning by an equally good breakfast of tea,
fruit, and cakes fried in butter. The next thing was
to sally forth in search of a home; and the first step
in the process was for Sandara to take out of a cupboard a highly ornamented wooden platter, cover it
with a sheet of pink paper, and then place upon it,
in formal array, four fine pears bought for the purpose,
which were afterwards covered with a silken scarf,
called in that country a *khata*, or scarf of blessings.

This khata is an implement-of-all-work in Thibetian
society. You pay visits with it, you ask or receive
favours with it, you enclose it in your letters when
you write—in short nothing can be done without the
presence and intervention of this little bit of thin
fringed silk, which is made to suit all pockets as to
price, seeing it is rigorously exacted from rich and
poor alike.

Its present use was to procure a lodging for the
party within the Lamasery, for which purpose it was
solemnly borne at the head of the little procession
by Sandara himself. It was quite effectual, for it
would have been the height of rudeness to refuse any

request so prefaced, and they speedily had assigned
to them a large room, having a comfortable kang, a
kitchen with cooking utensils, and stabling for the
beasts.

This Lamasery contains four thousand Lamas. It
is beautifully situated in a deep, well-wooded cleft in
the mountain-side, the white dwellings of the inmates
studding the slopes of the ravine, and climbing up
the face of the hill. Amid these modest homes are
seen uprising the gilded roofs of their temples, and
the turreted abodes of the chief Lamas, adorned by
floating streamers; while hither and thither flags are
displayed, inscribed with red or black mystic characters (which are also traced upon various parts of the
houses), and the odour of ever-burning incense diffuses
itself around. Red dresses and yellow mitres distin-
guish the Lamas, who stalk silently along the street
to their schools, or to the public prayer; while ani-
mation is given to the scene by the frequent caravans
of pilgrims arriving or departing after their pious
visit to this particularly holy place.

One of the most notable festivals celebrated at
Kounboum is that of the Flowers, which takes place
in January. This is simply an exhibition of modelled
work, secular and religious subjects, moulded in
butter. Our travellers were just in time for it, and
a curious sight it was.

Issuing from their house after nightfall, they beheld
innumerable bas-reliefs, representing, with exquisite
fidelity to nature, men of various nations, each in
their appropriate costumes. Mongols, Chinese, Tartars, Thibetians, and even a few Hindoos and negroes,

were here to be seen, each one discriminated from the other, however slight might be the difference of feature. Beasts of various kinds,—sheep, tigers, wolves, foxes—all in butter,—whose furs were rendered in the most life-like manner, were also included in these strange works of art; while battle pieces, hunting scenes, bits of pastoral life, with views of the chief Lamaseries of the empire, wrought out of the same singular material, presented themselves, as the visitors passed, wondering and admiring, from one temple to another. Further, there was a whole puppet-show of manikins, a foot high, who stalked along and disappeared from the stage—in butter. They were all beautifully moulded, the product of three months' labour of twenty of the most accomplished artists of the Lamasery: hard work, and cold work too, the hands requiring to be continually dipped in cold water, to prevent their warmth slurring the design.

The butter is first well kneaded, and then the frozen fingers go deftly to work, one artist completing one portion, another a second, of each design, and afterwards joining them into a whole under the superintending artist who has devised it.

While gazing on these wonderful and fragile productions, a hideous blare of conch-shells sounded in their ears. This was understood to herald the approach of the Head Lama, on his way to inspect the handiwork of his subjects, and who, preceded by Lamas armed with whips to clear the way, now made his important appearance. He was a man of about forty, middle sized, with a flat, common, unpleasantly-

complexioned face. He was clad in a purple silk
mantle, clasped on the chest after the manner of a
prelate's cope; wore a tall mitre, very like a fool's
cap; and carried a kind of crosier or pastoral staff.
He looked languidly at the beautiful objects around
him, and having received the respectful greetings of
the Tartars, returned to the Lamasery, leaving the
crowd in an uproar of merriment. The show was
soon at an end, for this amazing display of skill and
patience was the glorification of but a single night;
next morning not a trace of it was to be seen, every
morsel of butter having been thrown into a hollow
of the mountain, where the crows had their fill of it!

The subjects of study at this great seminary of
Buddhist learning are theology and medicine; and
the students are literally under an iron rule, seeing
that at lecture and at prayers they are superintended
by officials who, on the slightest provocation, deal
them blows with an iron rod kept for the purpose.
The theology is, of course, all connected with the
worship of Buddha. Their medical science sums up
four hundred and forty ways of being ill!

Study, however, is not the sole occupation of the
Lamas, who earn their own living in various ways.
Some sell the produce of their cows; some are arti-
ficers—tailors, bootmakers, hatters, to the community;
others manage the refreshment department, which, as
there are four thousand of them to be provided for,
is no sinecure; while printing and transcribing books,
the latter beautifully executed, form the occupation
of another class. Their writing is done with bam-
boos, shaped like our pens; the ink is contained in

small copper boxes filled, as with us before steel pens
came into fashion, with cotton wool. Water, with
one-tenth part of milk, is the simple and very efficient
size used to prevent the spreading of the ink upon
the paper.

In addition to the Festival of Flowers, the inhabitants of the Lamasery have others which may be called
" movable feasts," as they depend upon the generosity
of pilgrims or munificent brethren, who may take it
into their heads to treat the four thousand with tea.
In this case the feast is denominated a tea-general ;
if only certain portions of the community are invited,
it is then known as a tea-special.

When a tea-general is to be held, the announcement
is made on the conclusion of morning prayers. The
company present all remain sitting, while forty of the
young students bring from the kitchen great jars of
tea and milk, from which each guest is helped, generally twice, in his own wooden cup. A little butter
for each is sometimes added ; and if the entertainment
is to be one of unusual magnificence, oat-meal cakes.
When all have finished, the presiding Lama solemnly
announces the name of the giver of the refection,
who, at this juncture, drops down somewhat in the
manner of a frog; the assembled company sing a
hymn in his praise, and then march forth in procession ; after which the gratified host picks himself
up from the ground and retires also. A tea-drinking
of this kind, without either butter or oatmeal, sometimes costs about twenty pounds.

One young student of medicine, at Kounboum, gave
the missionaries great hopes of his conversion, by the

interest which he evidently took in their religious in-
structions. He was a good-natured fellow, always
ready to help them in their little difficulties in learning
the language, when Sandara the Bearded, whose duty
it was, was too ill-tempered to take the trouble of doing
so ; but he had not courage to avow his belief of the
Christian religion. He fancied he might be at the same
time a good Buddhist and a good Christian ; so he
prayed both to God and to his Buddhic deity, sometimes, with all simplicity, inviting the fathers to join in
these latter devotions. He one day begged them to
unite with him in a special act of religious charity, for
the providing poor travellers at a distance with horses.
The missionaries replied that this was, without doubt,
a good work, but as they were poor men themselves,
it was impossible for them to have the pleasure of
aiding him in his benevolent deed. That objection, he
answered, was not at all to the point, as the horses
thus sent were paper horses ; that is, slips of paper
with the figure of a galloping horse, ready bridled
and saddled, depicted on them—and which, being
thrown up into the air, after certain prayers, were
blown away by the wind, and turned into horses for
those who needed them. They replied, that as this
involved an appeal to Buddha, and a reliance upon
his power, they could not possibly have anything to do
with the matter; and he agreed with them. Nevertheless, he spent a good part of the night in making
a great number of these paper horses, which, next
day, in company of some friends, he carried off to a
certain mountain for the purpose of sending them on
their aerial journey.

It blew a hurricane that day, at noon ensued a snow-storm, and at night, chilled and worn out, the poor fellow returned to his friends, who recruited him with tea and bread, and inquired how he had succeeded in his enterprise. He admitted it had been a dreadful day; nevertheless, it had been a most favourable one for his purpose, as, on throwing his horses up into the air, a gust of wind had instantly whisked them away to every quarter of the globe : had he delayed at all, the papers would have been so damped by the snow, that they would have had no chance of rising. The twenty-fifth day of the month is the one appropriated to this singular act of devotion.

The removal of the two Abbés was, however, now at hand. The cause of this was the inflexible rule of the monastery, that all its inmates, mere passers through excepted, should wear the sacred dress of the Lamas ; and this, as a matter of conscience, the missionaries could not do. So, with all kindly courtesy, they were requested to betake themselves to a neighbouring Lamasery, where, the rules being less stringent, they might dress as they pleased.

A khata and a dish of raisins procured them as hospitable a reception at Tchogortan as they had already experienced at Kounboum, and within its walls they accordingly took up their abode for a while.

CHAPTER VI.

NOMADIC LIFE—A CARAVAN.

CHANGE of work is said to be as good as play. Thanks to Samdadchiemba's laziness, the good fathers enjoyed this at Tchogortan ; for, finding their beasts half starved through his neglect, who preferred prowling about the tents and drinking tea, to seeking out proper pasture for his charge, they diversified their learned labours by playing the herdsman, much to the advantage of the poor neglected animals.

The Eastern Thibetians, among whom they were now sojourning, are an exclusively pastoral people, living in rickety, shivery tents of black linen, about which, when encamped for any length of time, they erect a stone wall four or five feet high, and even construct a furnace within the uncomfortable dwelling; the whole of which is demolished without the slightest scruple when their vagrant taste urges a change, the stones being carried off for future use. They also do a little trade in hair and wool, and weave the coarse linen of which their tents are made.

Their herds consist of sheep, goats, and long-haired cattle of a peculiar kind, of which we give an illustration. The meat of the *yak*, which is its

Thibetian name, is excellent; so is the milk; much more so the butter. But the cows are difficult to deal with, as but for their good will not a drop of milk should any one get except their own calves.

LONG-HAIRED OX OR YAK

Their cunning owners manage them for all that. One cow, which had lost her own calf, was cleverly circumvented by having presented to her a very tolerable make-believe one stuffed with hay. She stared at it, sneezed contemplatively several times, and then licked it pleasantly, while her master was milking her; and when the make-believe accidentally came to pieces during the operation, subsiding into a mere bunch of hay, she equally pleasantly ate it up. That cow was a philosopher.

For variety of employment, the fathers here betook themselves to making ropes of the hair which
their camels, in "moulting," had shed abundantly.
Samdadchiemba looked on with mild superciliousness, and at length broke silence by asking his
"spiritual fathers" how it was that they degraded
themselves with such work; for he thought it very
undignified for clergymen to exercise any handicraft. The answer was prompt and to the point :
St. Paul himself "laboured with his hands," that
he might not be chargeable to those whom he
came to instruct. This was news to their critical
servant; and no sooner did he learn it than he took
up the trade himself, throwing his energies into
the rope making, not only with the utmost zeal, but
with great skill also; for, in truth, he was an old
hand at the business, though he had not thought it
needful to advert to that part of the matter while
he was under the impression that to work with the
hands was so intensely derogatory to any one's dignity.

The inhabitants of the valley in which this
Lamasery is situated live in such continual fear of
brigands that an armed watch is kept up to ward
off the marauders; and as at this time alarming
rumours, of their advance began to prevail, it became needful for the superior Lama of Kounboum
to take precautionary measures. For this purpose
a Grand Lama, accompanied by twenty students of
the Faculty of Prayers, climbed the loftiest mountain
at hand, and erecting their tents on its crest, proceeded to recite prayers to a musical accompani-

ment. Two days were spent in this exercise, in
performing a species of exorcism, and in building
an earthen cone, which was white-washed and surmounted by a flag inscribed with certain prayers.
This was called the Pyramid of Peace; and the whole
process being considered fully adequate to the pro-

PYRAMID OF PEACE.

tection of the valley and its frightened people against
all hostile attack, the reverend party marched down
the hill again, and returned to their seclusion.

But now there was joyful news of the approach of
the Thibetian embassy for which the missionaries
were waiting to convoy them to Lha-Ssa. It was
expected to be a four months' journey thither, and
provision had to be made beforehand, as there was

small chance of finding any on the road. Four bricks
of tea, two sheep's paunches of butter, two sacks of
flour, and eight of barley-meal, there called *tsamba*,
were found requisite for this purpose, and they re-
paired to Kounboum to procure them. The barley-
meal is used to mix with hot tea into a kind of
wretched stir-about, or hasty pudding, neither hot nor
cold, cooked nor raw, but which is duly eaten by the
Thibetians for breakfast, dinner, or supper, according
to the time of day when it is taken. This Spartan diet
was to be the grand resource of the travellers; and
having bought another camel and horse, and hired an
adjutant to Samdadchiemba, the party moved off. The
Blue Lake, or Sea, for its vast area of waters merits
rather the latter title, was their destination, there to
await the embassy.

It was nearly a month before it arrived. Two thousand men, some on horseback, armed with spears,
swords, guns, bows and arrows, some on camels, some
on foot, some mounted on oxen; twelve hundred
camels, twelve hundred horses, fifteen hundred of the
yak, or long-haired cattle; the Tchanak-Kampo, or
Grand Lama himself, in a litter borne between two
mules; and a guard of five hundred soldiers, partly
Chinese, partly Tartars;—such was the composition
of this monstrous caravan setting out on a four months'
journey through the ineffable wilds of far-off Thibet.

The order of proceeding was thus: each day a cannon-shot, two or three hours before dawn, woke the
sleepers, who jumped up, lighted their fires, boiled
innumerable kettles, and then made illimitable tea,
which was swallowed along with the delicate mess of

barley-meal already described. Breakfast over, the
tents were struck, and at a second cannon-shot the
march began, a few wary horsemen heading it, followed by interminable strings of camels : to them
succeeded the cattle in detachments of two or three

THE TCHANAK-KAMPO, AND THE CARAVAN.

hundred, each under the care of several herdsmen;
while the cavalry of the party advanced at their own
sweet will, capering here and there according to their
taste. So huge a procession could not get along
noiselessly, and the sound of their progress was a
composite one, consisting of doleful voice of camels,
bellowing of bulls, meek lowing of kine, neighing of
horses, jingling of camel-bells, and the varied human
voice, bass and treble, of the travellers. The day's
progress ended, tents were pitched for the night, struck
next morning, and so the process was repeated on and

on westward, yet slightly sloping south, from the
Blue Sea.

It was sometimes very pleasant, at other times
very disagreeable; especially when it came to flounder-
ing in the ice, as the thousands crossed a half-frozen
river emptying itself into the Blue Lake. And yet it
was reckoned a successful passage of that same stream,
seeing that only one man broke his legs, and only
two beasts were drowned therein.

The route through the Desert of Thibet was a trying and hazardous one. Fear of being murdered by
robbers gave way to fear of being killed by the cold;
and beast after beast had to be abandoned to its sad
fate as the caravan toiled on amid the scattered bones
of their predecessors in this dreary journey. Snow,
wind, and cold, altogether, were almost too much even
for our travellers. The hot barley-meal paste prepared in the morning for the day's sustenance, placed
in the bosom for warmth, and covered over with furs
and woollens, was yet so frozen as to risk breaking
their teeth while meagerly satisfying their mid-day
hunger. Horses and mules had to be muffled up
in carpeting until they were laughable to look at,
and yet a tenth of them died of cold; and what was
worse, even human beings, whom it was impossible
to save, had to be left by the chill road-side freezing
into slow death.

It was a horrible journey, but it came to an end
at last, and on the 29th of January 1846, the setting
sun saw our travellers in sight of Lha-Ssa, the capital
of Buddhism, and night fell upon them lodged within
its bounds.

CHAPTER VII.

LHA-SSA, the capital of Thibet, is a city about two leagues in circumference, containing a mixed population of Thibetians, Indians from Boutan, Mussulmans from Cashmere, and Chinese, amounting to about 80,000. The meaning of the name is, the Land of Spirits. It has good streets, sufficiently clean in dry weather, and houses several stories high, built of stone, brick, or mud, all white-washed to distraction, and ornamented with a streak of the sacred colours, yellow and red, round door and window : the insides of these houses are dirty, smoky, and ill-smelling in the extreme. Its Buddhist temples exceed in size and richness of decoration those of any other city of the empire. The suburbs are verdurous, abounding in gardens with beautiful trees; but the dwellings are abominably dirty. In one quarter the houses are singularly constructed of the horns of sheep and oxen, great numbers of which are devoured by the beef-and-mutton-loving grandees of the place: the smooth white horns of the oxen are interspersed in various devices with the rough black ones of the sheep, and the spaces filled up with mortar. These are the only houses that escape the universal whitewashing, and they have rather a picturesque appearance.

About a mile north of the town stands the palace of the Telé, or Delai Lama, the spiritual head, not only of Thibet, but of great part of Eastern Asia, given up to the worship of Buddha. It is erected on a rugged rising ground, and is a congeries of temples: the centre one, rich with barbaric gold, overlooks the rest, and is the special abode of this human divinity. Two avenues of stately trees give access to it from the city, and are thronged with pilgrims from all quarters of the Buddhic world, together with court attendants in befitting costume, and bestriding finely-trapped horses.

The town itself is as busy as other great capitals—commerce and devotion divide the interest of the place, and both are keenly pursued. The Thibetians have a Chinese style of face, are middle-sized, supple, strong, brave, and religious after their manner. They walk about jantily, humming a tune, dress handsomely, but do not care much about washing themselves. Their costume consists of an ample garment, girded with a red sash; red or purple cloth boots; and a blue, red-tufted cap, bordered with black velvet. For dress occasions, a large red hat, fringed, is substituted for this cap. A bag containing the wooden cup, which in this country is breakfast, dinner, and tea service all in one, is suspended from the girdle, as are also two small embroidered ones for show, not for use. The hair is worn long and flowing, occasionally braided into tails, and ornamented with precious stones. As to their manners, it may suffice to say

that in Thibet the correct mode of paying your respects
to your friends is, to take off your hat, stick out your
tongue at them, and scratch your right ear. These

VIEW OF LHA-SSA.

three movements simultaneously executed have a very
graceful effect, and are reckoned intensely polite.

The dress of the women is not very unlike that of
the men, only that over the robe is worn a short party-
coloured coat; the hair is braided into two tails, and

a small, yellow, conical cap is the head-dress in humble life—the great ladies have a kind of pearl coronet. All, as a finishing touch to their personal appearance, when they go out of doors, rub their faces over with a black, sticky mess like jelly; those who put on the greatest quantity being reputed the most pious, and, we presume, the most fashionable also. They enjoy, however, a greater amount of liberty in going abroad than do most Asiatic women. Perhaps the black varnish is supposed to render this safe. They are stirring and industrious, both in-doors and out, following various little trades, or toil-ing as farm-servants in the country.

The men are passably diligent in their different callings of spinning and weaving, and in various manufactures, including excellent pottery.

Owing to the nature of the country, covered with mountains, and intersected by rushing torrents, agri-culture is not very productive. Little wheat or rice is grown; black barley, upon which every one mainly lives, is the staple of their fields. Animal food and fish, both of which are good, are eaten only by the higher classes, and then as a dainty course by itself—like game with us—two plates, one of boiled, the other of raw meat, being served on such occasions, and eaten with equal satisfaction. Their repasts are washed down with an acid ale. Gold and silver are abundant in the soil, but, as usual, the masses of the population are none the richer for that.

Like the rest of the world, the Thibetians of Lha-Ssa make great festival of the New Year. The last days of the old year are spent in dusting, rubbing,

and cleaning, laying in stores of eatables and drink-
ables, painting up their household idols, and forming
ornaments in butter to deck their shrines.   The moment that midnight has passed, the whole town breaks
out into a frantic expression of joy, heightened by
bells, tambourines, and the other noisy items of
Thibetian music.   Then people rush about carrying

THIBETIAN THEATRE.

small earthen vessels full of hot water, in which float
little sweetmeat balls of flour and honey, which are
hooked for with a slender silver implement by those
to whom the basin is presented.   It is impossible to
reject this polite attention, especially when it is offered
with the tongue stuck out in the most friendly and
winning manner.   This is the sport of the night.
When day dawns, the honey-pots are exchanged for

tea-pots full of buttered tea, which are carried in one hand, while the other sustains a mighty platter of barley-meal; and it is incumbent upon those to whom it is tendered to drink a cup of tea and eat a pinch of meal. Dances and songs amuse the day, while in open spaces theatrical entertainments attract the populace. The performances consist chiefly of dancing and tumbling, and other antics, executed with more spirit than grace by the grotesquely costumed actors.

The Boutan Indians who live in this city have all the working of metals in their hands, be it rough iron-work or delicate goldsmith-ware. They are a slight, active, dark-complexioned race, with cunning little black eyes. Their peculiarity is to wear a dab of dark red paint on the forehead, put on fresh every morning. The Mussulmans, or Katchi, are the great merchants: some of them even proceed to Calcutta for the transaction of business, no other Thibetian subjects being permitted to do so. The Chinese are chiefly soldiers—a guard for their ambassador, and official persons—and little love is lost between them and the natives. They are regarded with suspicion, as being encroaching, under pretence of deep respect for the Telé Lama. On one occasion an old grudge between the two broke out into open violence. The two resident Chinese ambassadors had made themselves especially obnoxious by their interference in state affairs, and the matter issued in the assassination of the Thibetian governor, who had set himself in opposition to the designs of the two. A native who was on the spot, snatched up the head of the

murdered man, placed it on a pike, and rushed with
it through the streets invoking vengeance on the
Chinese. The population was readily raised, and
thronging tumultuously to the palace of the ambassadors, tore them in pieces upon the spot; nor did

INSURRECTION OF THE THIBETIANS AT LHA-SSA.

they stay until all the Chinese they could lay hands
on throughout the empire had been pitilessly slain.
War ensued between the two countries; the Chinese
had the worst of it in fighting, but in talking secured
the advantage, so that things went on again as before,
a small Chinese garrison being stationed here and there

in the land. In Lha-Ssa they are hated, despised, and laughed at, by the rest of the citizens.

But it was time for our travellers to settle, now that they had reached the termination of their journey. Two rooms, at the very top of a house containing fifty lodgers, were accordingly engaged by them for their residence at Lha-Ssa. Twenty-six break-neck steps, that for safety's sake had to be ascended on hands and knees, led to them. The larger room, which they kept for their own use, had a window with strong wooden bars, and a hole in the roof to let in light, rain, snow, wind, and let out the smoke of their fire, kindled on the floor in a glazed earthen-ware pan. Its furniture consisted of two goat-skins, by way of bed, on the floor; their tent; some old boots and portmanteaus; three ragged robes; a bundle of night-clothes; and a stock of fuel in the corner. The smaller apartment was furnished with a brick stove for cooking; and here Samdadchiemba reigned supreme. The horses, lean enough after the hardships of their four months' journey, were stabled in the court.

Sallying out to make some purchases, the friends entered a cup shop, to replace their well-worn cups-of-all-work. These cups are made of the root of certain native trees, and are well shaped, ornamented only with a transparent varnish that shows all the natural markings of the wood; and yet they vary in price from two or three small coins to forty pounds of our money. Making known their wants, the well-blacked shop-woman handed them two cups, politely informing them that the price of each was fifty ounces of silver—equivalent to twenty pounds. This was rather overwhelming; but at length a pair was found for which they disbursed

THIBETIAN CUP SHOP.

one ounce of silver; and, when they got home, had the satisfaction of being told by their landlord that they ought to have had four such for the money.

Our travellers found themselves much at their ease in the Thibetian capital; for, with all their faults, the natives are fifty times pleasanter to deal with than the Chinese. They were duly recognized as foreigners, officially, according to custom, by an indifferent head of police, who, after taking down their statement, wiped his pen in his hair, and coolly said, "Very well :" in return for which, with true Thibetian politeness, they put out their tongues at him, departed, and there was an end of it—for a time.

But they had not long given themselves up to the good work, for the sake of which they had undertaken their perilous mission to the centre of Buddhism, when trouble came upon them in this wise : A well-dressed Chinese one day called upon them, and after talking and fussing, himself, and four subsequent officials, the missionaries were pounced upon as spies, and carried off for examination before the Regent of Thibet, a majestic-looking, highly-intelligent personage, of some fifty years of age, clad in a furred yellow robe, wearing a diamond ear-ring, and having his long black hair fastened by three gold combs : his cap, orna-mented with precious stones, lay on a green cushion at his side.

He looked pleasant when they appeared before him, questioned them, and finding they were not particularly ready in speaking his own tongue, desired them to write something in their own. One of the two, ever faithful to their supreme design of impart-ing eternal truth to this people, thereupon wrote in French these words : "What can it profit a man to gain the whole world, if he lose his own soul?" The characters were new to the Regent, and he desired they should be translated ; which was done into Thibetian, Chinese, and the Tartar language. The Regent read and pondered the translation, slowly repeating to himself the impressive words, which he pronounced to be as profound as any in their own prayer-books. At this juncture, to their annoyance, that old fox the Chinese ambassador made his appearance; and the Regent, handing them over to him, with a reassuring intimation that he himself was their friend, took his departure.

Remembering with what bitter persecution the Chinese authorities had treated other Christians, it was rather an alarming state of things for the good fathers. But their trust in the goodness of God was unshaken; and relying on that promise of their Lord, that when brought before kings and governors for His sake, words should be given to His faithful followers, they calmly awaited the interview. Even Samdadchiemba, uncouth, troublesome youth as he was, rose to the occasion, and firmly resolved on abiding by his profession of Christianity, whatever came of it.

The ambassador proved to be Ki-chan, successor to the notable Commissioner Lin, whose folly originally provoked the war between England and China. He questioned and cross-questioned both the missionaries and their servant, and then dismissed them to the supper provided for them by their good friend the Regent in his own house. Soundly frightened as they had been, it had not taken away their appetites, so that the meal was very acceptable; and after conversing with the great man far into the night, they retired to the sleeping-room prepared for their use while in custody—for that was precisely what they were. They would fain have slept, but the boundless curiosity of the Lamas, who kept popping in and out like rabbits in a warren, in order to stare at them, effectually prevented this. Tired out at last, they ventured to tell their tormentors that they were going to bed, and wished to be left alone. The information was received politely, nay, some were even so very well bred as to put out their tongues at them in reply, but stir they would not; they evidently were anxious to see in what manner learned Europeans put themselves to bed. As there was no getting rid of them, the fathers at last knelt down to say their prayers, concluding by once more entreating the gazers to be gone, and as the request was enforced by putting out the light, compliance was unavoidable; so, with a good-natured laugh, their tormentors groped their way out in the dark.

It was a great relief to be left alone after the agitating events of the day; yet what the morrow might bring forth—freedom or death—it was impossible to foretell. But these good men calmed their anxieties by steadfast reliance upon God, without whom, they knew, not a hair of their heads should fall.

The speedy dawn gave them a visit from the governor of the Katchi, a Mussulman, resident in Lha-Ssa, with whom they had already had a friendly meeting in the Regent's palace, and who now brought them fruit and cakes, with a kindly inquiry after their welfare.

He was a young man for so important a post, being only thirty-two, with a good candid face. He and the Regent were friends, and both were determined, if possible, to rescue the missionaries from the clutches

of the powerful Chinese, to whose ill-will their present
difficulties were owing.   The governor gave them
some useful advice for their coming interview with
Ki-chan, and then took his departure, leaving them

GOVERNOR OF THE KATCHI.

to breakfast upon his cakes and fruit, for which they
felt more inclination than for the more elaborate
meal of buttered tea, with the proper solid accom-
paniments, sent them by the Regent.

When they were again presented before the great

man, their whole possessions were officially sealed up, and then carried in formal procession to the tribunal, where the Chinese ambassador was awaiting them. Two old trunks contained the worldly goods of the missionaries, and after the seals had been broken, their simple contents were displayed, to the effectual clearing of their character, as it seemed, for the Tartars thereupon respectfully put out their tongues and scratched their ears at them, while the Chinese made them impressive bows : better still, they were dismissed, trunks and all, in freedom to their own lodgings ! There the good governor soon followed them with dinner, carried by his servant ; and when they inquired, in some dismay, about their horses, which had vanished during their absence, he told them the animals were well cared for in the Regent's stables, and that he was commissioned to buy them for his highness ; laying down, as he spoke, a superabundant price, which they in vain entreated him to diminish. So all ended well ; Samdadchiemba, who shared the good fortune of his kind masters, emphatically pronouncing it "a happy day."

The next day was happier still, for their friend the Regent, remarking how badly they were lodged, frankly invited them to take up their abode in one of his houses. They duly inducted themselves therein, and rejoiced, not only in the added comfort, but in the freedom which they now experienced to worship God publicly, without let or hindrance, in the capital of Buddhism.

But their old friend Ki-chan had not yet done with them, and they soon became aware that he was plotting to get them removed, not only from the capital, but from Thibet itself.

The attack was opened by the ambassador's send-

MILITARY MANDARIN.

ing for the missionaries, and, after a little canting and coaxing, telling them that Thibet was too poor a country for them, they had better go home to France.

He was met with spirit, and informed that as they had permission from the Thibetian government to reside in Lha-Ssa, they did not recognize any authority on his part to send them away. Some discussion ensued, the end of which was, that the Chinese coolly told them he would make them leave. And he was as good as his word; for, after much ado, the Regent not being particularly disposed to let his Chinese masters ride over him rough-shod in this way, his guests felt themselves obliged to comply with Ki-chan's wish, and they notified the same to their friend, who, sorry as he was, admitted that he did not think it prudent point-blank to resist the powerful Chinese.

When their decision was communicated to Ki-chan, he said it was best for all parties that they should leave the country; and he had already made arrangements for their journey back, maliciously selecting for this purpose the longest and most round-about route, occupying eight months. They were to travel under the care of a military mandarin, who, with his followers, would set out in eight days' time. Remonstrance was vain, and after protesting against his doings, the missionaries were forced to comply with them.

A friendly leave-taking with the Regent followed. He could not help himself; he dared not thwart his powerful friend and master, the Emperor of China, in the person of his ambassador. On their return home, they found the good Katchi with presents of travelling stores, and he insisted on staying all evening to help them to pack. Samdadchiemba, as a

Chinese subject, they were reluctantly compelled to part with; but the friendly Regent provided for him also. Indeed, Ki-chan promised that the youth should come to no harm; and he kept his promise.

The day of departure came. The mandarin in

LAST INTERVIEW WITH KI-CHAN.

whose charge they were to travel invited them to an excellent breakfast; and when that was over, they accompanied him and his escort to take leave of the ambassador.

On entering his apartment, the soldiers did him

lowly obeisance, by throwing themselves on the floor, like so many frogs, and knocking it with their foreheads. The mandarin did the same, but being very infirm through much brandy-drinking, had to be helped up and set on his legs again by his companions. The missionaries paid their respects in more civilized style.

Ki-chan had something to say to each one, beginning politely with his victims the missionaries, and winding up with a terrific "obey and tremble" to the fifteen soldiers, who grovelled with their noses in the dust before him. Finally, he committed some valuable property, which he wished conveyed to China, to the special care of the men he was driving out of the country. Why he should prefer confiding in the oppressed Christians to trusting his own countrymen he best knew.

Mounting the horses provided for them, the party proceeded through the streets, staying a moment outside the town to give a few words of encouragement to those Thibetians who had listened with interest to their Christian teaching, and who now awaited them in a body. Exhortations to abandon their heathen practices, to worship, and put full trust in the infinite mercy of, the true God, made up the brief but pathetic address from their instructors. The friendly Katchi soon joined the travellers, riding with them to the frontiers, where, with a hearty shake of the hand, he took leave of them. Their last look at the city where they had hoped to win many souls to Christ, and which was now disappearing in the distance, was on the 15th of March 1846.

CHAPTER VIII.

IT was very provoking to be thus turned out of Thibet, after the extreme difficulty which the missionaries had experienced in getting into it; especially so now that they were settled, and found the people wonderfully willing to receive their Christian instruction. It was more than provoking: these good men felt it a severe trial to have to submit, in this matter, to that will of God concerning it which was directly opposed to their own.

But though somewhat ignominiously compelled to depart, they were treated with much respect by their convoy, and soon found the difference between journeying in these sterile lands as humble preachers of Christ's gospel, and as members of the travelling party of a Chinese mandarin.

His excellency Ly, Pacificator of Kingdoms—that was his lofty title at full length—was not prepossessing to look at. He was only forty-five years old, but might have been taken for seventy. His face was flabby and wrinkled, his eyes weak and dull, scanty gray hair surmounted his disagreeable counte-

nance, while his ungainly figure was quite a match
for the face and head. But he was rather a clever
man: he had seen the world, and noted it; talked
well; loved to discourse on philosophical and religious subjects. About his own particular faith he
was somewhat heedless; and as to the doctrine of
his new friends, scarcely knowing what it was, he
intimated he must be better acquainted with it before
he professed it. Further, he tried to make a fine
gentleman of himself; in which praiseworthy design
he sometimes failed. Such was the distinguished
individual under whose auspices they now travelled;
and thanks to whom, at their first resting-place, they
found themselves in a comfortable room, with a good
fire, and the luxury of buttered tea awaiting them, in
place of their old battered tent, to be set up with
their own hands, and then fuel to be sought before
they could prepare, perhaps, but a little tepid tea,
made of bad water, and stirred up with a pinch of
barley-meal by way of food. There was some advantage in being a species of state-prisoners. Here also
they were joined by a Grand Lama, whom their friend
the Regent had despatched to meet the travellers,
and see them comfortably out of his territories. He
brought with him two young men, whom he presented to them as attendants on the way, adding
that, as the missionaries were not used to Thibetian
food, it had been arranged that they should eat with
the mandarin, who was abundantly civil to his charge.

As to Thibetian cookery, when one learns that the
natives know no better than to boil pheasants and
partridges, and then eat them without seasoning, one

can sympathize with any Europeans who might be condemned to feed with them.

Stumbling, slipping, and sliding over evil roads, and no roads at all, sometimes dragged up almost perpendicular heights by holding on to the tails of their horses, their progress brought the travellers into a district where, according to a Chinese Road Book, lent them by their friend Ly, that "curious animal" the unicorn is still found. This strange creature, it is said, really exists in Thibet. Our travellers had not the good fortune to see one, but the people of this neighbourhood spoke of it as though not unfamiliar. It is said to be a graceful animal of the antelope species, its fur reddish-brown on the back, white on the lower part of the body. Its one long, somewhat curved, black horn is, of course, its most remarkable feature.

The glacier of the Mountain of Spirits proved a trying bit of road to the party. The beasts were sent at it first, a fine yak taking precedence. He put out his nose as if making an observation, smelt the ice, and giving a great puff, placed his fore-feet on the slippery ground, and was off like a shot, rolling over and over when he got to the bottom. One after another followed the bold adventurer, the horses rather more timidly, and the whole of that department of the cavalcade was safely landed. The men came next: sitting down on the ice, using their heels, close together, for a prow, they rapidly cut and slid their way down also. When all had thus descended, the horses were caught, and the procession resumed its way with varying fortune amid the doleful, frozen country, so rugged and mountainous that, in native speech, any

height short of being lost in the clouds is called a
plain, or a level road. One of these "level roads,"
which it was yet admitted required care to ascend, on
account of the path being narrow and slippery, it is

DEFILE OF ALAN-TO.

almost impossible to give an idea of in words; our
cut will do it more effectively. It shows a travelling
party crawling along a narrow path in the steep hill-
side, so narrow that often there is just room for

the horses' feet, while hidden depths, whence rise the sullen sound of waters, yawn beneath them. Where the path failed, a projecting ledge was formed of the trunks of trees, laid upon piles fixed in the earth. Three oxen came to an end in this dreadful abyss ; it was a mercy that as many men did not do the like.

This fearful defile conducted them to one of the pleasantest villages they had yet met with; situated in a fertile country, well watered and wooded. The houses here are constructed of trunks of trees, laid upon strong beams of timber driven into the earth: these form the floor. The walls are raised also of trees piled up one on the other. They are roofed with tree trunks and pieces of bark; so that they are regular wooden cages on a large scale. In one of them a few days' rest was had, whilst oxen were sent forward to trample down a path through the abundant snow with which a huge mountain, that of Tanda, lying in their way, was covered, and which would have been impassable by any other means.

The ascent began; but spite of the path tramped out for them, its difficulties, from combined wind and snow, were such that the Abbé Gabet was more dead than alive when they got to the top of it. Coming down again on the other side was equally difficult, so they just sat down and slid along till they got to the bottom. They felt somewhat in-dignant at old Ki-chan for having compelled them to take so wretched and dangerous a road.

The poor mandarin suffered much from this up-hill down-dale journey in frost, snow, and wind. When a few days' rest took place at a squalid city between

six and seven hundred miles on their way, he was in
such a state that medical advice had to be sought;
and the physicians, after examining his case, oracularly
gave it as their opinion that if his disorder diminished
it would not be of much importance, but if it increased
it might prove serious. He was recommended to
continue his journey in a palanquin, as he could not
get on or off his horse without several persons to
help him. But poor Ly had a passion for silver
ingots, and as the palanquin would have involved
the expenditure of no small quantity of these, he
evaded it by protesting his horse would weary him
much less. So he was once more hoisted into the
saddle, and their progress was resumed, the party
being increased by the addition of a picturesque group
of a Chinese soldier, with his Thibetian wife and
children, returning from service in Thibet, to settle
in his own country. The wife, with a baby fastened
knapsack-wise on her shoulders, bestrode a donkey,
leading a pack-horse with a couple of panniers,
out of which two children popped their little heads
merrily, the smaller of the two having a large
stone in his pannier, to keep the balance with his
heavier companion. The father followed on horseback, with a lad of twelve perched behind him. The
Chinese soldiers laughed at the man for bringing to
his own country a "large-footed woman," and so
many "little barbarians," surmising that he perhaps
intended to make money by exhibiting these "animals
of Thibet." It would have been more in keeping
with Chinese notions and customs, in these matters,
had he left them all behind, and settled himself snugly

to enjoy his savings alone. This was precisely what
the Pacificator of Kingdoms had done with his wife,
whose tears on the occasion (not very bitter ones)
had appeared to him utterly unreasonable, seeing he
had left her a comfortable house and provision.

Travelling with a mandarin of course usually procured for the party all needful attentions in the way
of beasts of burden and other accessories, which by
law are appropriated to such officers according to
their rank. But as they proceeded, even his awful
name was found to lose much of its power, and at
one stage the head man of the village waited upon
them to say that his people had made up their minds
not to perform the customary duties of this sort
without payment for them. He said this with
decision, and cut the matter short by at once making
his bow—that is, politely putting out his tongue at
them—and going his way. His insubordination was
alarming, more so to the mandarin than to the good
fathers, who would have had no particular objection
to being left behind in Thibet, since it was for that
purpose they had come there. In this emergency the
astounded Chinese determined on seeking the intervention of the chief Proul-Tamba, who lived some mile
or two off, and was a celebrity of the neighbourhood.

His messengers soon returned with news of the
approach of the chief, and each one brushed and
smartened himself up to do honour to the distinguished visitor. At last he made his appearance on
horseback; and entering the house, coolly took the
place of honour, as one accustomed to it, while the
travelling party arranged themselves around him.

He was a man of about forty, middle-sized, pale, thin face, lighted up by a pair of most lamp-like eyes, and wearing his black hair flowing about his shoulders. His dress was a voluminous green silk robe, trimmed with wolf-fur, and girded with a red belt; large

PROUL-TAMBA, A CELEBRATED THIBETIAN CHIEF.

purple leather boots, and a bushy fox-skin cap: he also wore a ponderous sword. After surveying his companions for a while, one of his servants distri-buted khatas among them, and then he spoke, telling the mandarin how much older he looked than when he (the speaker) last saw him. He added some-thing else equally uncivil; all of which the Chinese received with the most edifying humility. At length the depressed grandee ventured to refer to

(347)   8

the cause of his seeking an interview with Proul-Tamba, and was succinctly told that henceforth escort for the Chinese there would be none without payment; only, as he was an old acquaint-ance, and moreover was convoying two Lamas of the Western Heaven, who had been recommended to his protection by the Regent himself, for that once he should go scot-free. With that he called the recusant of the preceding evening, who, kneeling and respectfully putting his tongue in his cheek at him, received his commands to have the accustomed service in the matter of horses prepared immediately. Having invited the party to take tea with him in his own house, he then mounted his horse and rode off at a gallop.

The horses were soon at hand, and the cavalcade set out to visit the chief in his moated castle. A drawbridge admitted them, and they were ushered into a vast hall hung with various coloured flags, and whose roof was supported by ponderous gilded beams. Three large images of Buddha, having censers, and lamps fed with butter before them, stood at one end of the apartment. In a corner was a low table with red cushions. Here they were invited to seat themselves; the lady of the house, with well blacked face and jewelled tresses, soon making her appearance, carrying a tea-pot so big that it required both hands to hold it. Each guest had his cup filled with ex-cellent tea, topped with a thick coating of butter; and whilst they were drinking it she fetched two gilt wooden dishes, full of raisins and nuts. These were offered as something special, but the raisins proved mere rubbish, and the nuts could not be got out of the shell. Comfort was, however, in store for them, as this was only a prelude to an abundant dinner of kid and venison, with Thibetian beer to drink. Dinner ended, they took their leave, well pleased with the hospitality of Proul-Tamba and his well-blacked wife.

On resuming their march, the travellers were surprised to find that all their guides had left them, their places being filled by the women of the village. The explanation given was amusing: they were approaching an unfriendly village, the people of which would certainly have come out to fight the *men* accompanying the cavalcade, and in that case their beasts would have become the property of the conquerors. Fond of fighting, however, as the men of Gaya were, they were much too chivalric to attack women;—to do so would disgrace them throughout the whole Thibetian world. The wisdom of this abdication in favour of the women was soon apparent. On drawing near the warlike village, out pranced a formidable body of well-armed horsemen, making unmistakable warlike demonstrations, but who set up a tremendous laugh when they saw that the caravan was headed by women; though they did not fail to indulge in some contemptuous remarks upon the men who had thus saved themselves by putting their wives and daughters foremost. The lady-guides took it coolly, and having refreshed themselves with buttered tea, at once returned in triumph with the beasts their adroitness had preserved from the enemy.

CHAPTER IX.

THE pleasant climate of Bathang, a district that divides the frontiers of Thibet and China, afforded the travellers a few days' rest, which was much needed, especially by poor Ly, whose case was becoming serious. His rapid decline had not been unnoticed by the missionaries, who sought to impress upon the dying man, with reference to his own soul, those great truths of Christianity which had been discussed between them by the way. He listened attentively, assented to what they said, admitted his own belief of the doctrines which had been taught him, and that it was incumbent upon all to embrace them. But when urged to do this himself, there was a hesitation. He must, he said, delay it until he had reached his own family and resigned his rank as mandarin: it was absolutely impossible for him to serve the Lord of Heaven whilst he remained a mandarin of the Emperor. There was no getting that idea out of his head; so Ly, like some others, deferred it to a more convenient season—one that, alas! never arrived.

Two or three days' further travel brought them to a dull little village, where having rested for the night,

they rose and strolled about next morning, previous
to resuming their march. The prospect was attrac-
tive, the sky clear and bright, as the sun looked at
them over the horizon; everything was cheering when
they returned to take their place in the caravan,
which was drawn up in order for the start—the men,
whip in hand, standing by their horses, awaiting the
signal to mount. The two hastened on with some
remark about their being late, but were told by one
of the soldiers there was no hurry, as the mandarin
had not yet opened his door. He was desired to call
his master; but on entering, poor Ly was found dying
on his bed, and a few moments left them with only
the corpse of their protector, who, they were fain to
hope, might, even in his last solitary hour, have
thrown himself upon the mercy of that God in whose
nature he had been instructed, and who "will have
all men to be saved."

A short delay ensued on this melancholy event;
and the cavalcade resumed its progress, bearing with
it (covered with a white pall, which is supposed to
conduce to the happiness of the deceased) the body
of the poor mandarin to its last resting-place.

It was embarrassing to find a travelling party of this
size, and, with the exception of the two Frenchmen,
composed of what we call half civilized people, left
without commander. If every man of these Thibetians
and Chinese had been left to do what was right in
his own eyes, the result would have been what was
wrong in those of everybody else. The missionaries
felt this difficulty keenly, and of sheer necessity appointed themselves a provisional government until

they should obtain some authorized leader. An opportunity for this soon occurred. On arriving at the station of Lithang (that means, Copper Plain), they earnestly requested that one of the four mandarins in charge there, should assume the place of Ly. This was objected to : not one of the gentlemen could spare himself for the unpleasant service. But the Frenchmen were not going to be checkmated by a set of Chinese. On receiving their refusal to accompany them, they replied that in that case they should go where they pleased ; possibly they might think fit to return to Lha-Ssa. This was alarming, and elicited from the officials an immediate response, that they would think about it. The mandarins did think about it, and to such purpose, that in the evening Pa-Tsoung, one of the four, presented himself in full dress to inform them that he was to have the unexpected honour of leading the party to its destination. This was very good, and as, under the courteous pretext of giving them time to recruit, the mandarin required a couple of days to get himself ready for the journey, they had time to look about them a little.

It was a kind of transition district, not exactly Thibet, not exactly China : the natives were more polite, and also more grasping and cunning, than those of the former country. Further, the language differed so greatly, that the Thibetians pure, could with difficulty understand it. The costume was the same as in the interior, with the exception of the head-gear. The women surmounted their flowing tresses with a flat piece of silver, like a dinner plate, and they did not black their faces. The town itself is situated in a dreary, barren plain, which yields only a little barley, and miserable herbs.

The mandarin having arranged his affairs, the caravan once more got under weigh, the garrison presenting arms, and, with military etiquette, wishing "health and prosperity" to the pale, inanimate form borne to its long rest among them. The new leader returned thanks in the name of the dead man, and then they rode off. He was an insignificant-looking little being, and turned out not only an insatiable talker, but an excessive bore.

The remainder of the road proved like its beginning, rugged and mountainous in the extreme ; and though the month was June, the very last inch of Thibet *snowed* them into China, as they entered the frontier town of the Forge of Arrows.

The duties of their Thibetian escort being now at an end, its members returned to their own country, bearing with them letters of heartfelt thanks to the Regent of Lha-Ssa for the kindly care he had bestowed upon those whom the necessities of his position, not his own will, had led him to expel from his territories.

The missionaries remained a few days in this town, and after repeated quarrels with the resident mandarins, at length obtained the consent of those sublime personages to their finishing their journey in palanquins ; for in truth they were utterly worn out with their three months on horseback. Their destination was Tching-tou-fou, the capital of the western province of Sse-Tchouen, and formerly one of the finest cities of the empire, until knocked to pieces by civil war in the seventeenth century. In this city they were to undergo a kind of trial by a jury of mandarins appointed by the Sacred Master. The result of it was a prohibition of their remaining in China, across which they were therefore conducted to Macao, a Portuguese island-settlement close on its south-east coast. Gabet hastened home to complain to the French Government of the treatment which he and his companion had received from the Chinese authorities. The Abbé Huc appears to have remained in Macao for some time, employing a portion of his much needed rest and leisure in preparing for publication those recollections of his travels which have furnished materials for our little volume.

20820-11